Published with the assistance of WordF

MGs,
the MINI
and ME

Dudley Pike

Copyright © Dudley Pike 2015

ISBN 13: 978-1508778516

ISBN 10: 1508778515

ALL RIGHTS RESERVED

This book is a work of non-fiction based on the life, experiences, and recollections of Dudley Pike. In some cases names, places, dates, sequences, or the details of events may have been changed to protect the privacy of others. The author has stated to the publishers that except in such minor respects not affecting the substantial accuracy of the work the contents of this book are true to the very best of his recollection.

The right of the author to be identified as the author of this work has been asserted by him in accordance with the relevant copyright legislations in her country of residence and generally under section 6bis of the Berne Convention for the Protection of Literary and Artistic Works.

This book may not by way of trade or otherwise be lent, resold, hired out, reproduced, or otherwise circulated without the prior consent of the publisher or author.

(Images courtesy of the author except where otherwise stated)

For enquiries about rights or volume sales, please contact Dudley Pike by email:

dpike01@gmail.com

Published with the assistance of WordPlay Publishing Ltd.

This book is dedicated to my father who died suddenly at the age of 58, when I was 20 years old. I openly admit that I've missed him tremendously from the moment he passed away and throughout my life, and wish I'd had the opportunity to know him better. The lack of father-son moments over the years probably affected the relationships I have with my own sons and the way that I have behaved towards them.

This book is also dedicated to them, my two wonderful sons. I admit I wasn't a great father and words cannot express my regret in letting them both down and not being there during those important early years when a child needs both its parents. Thankfully, we enjoy a super relationship now; and I love my sons and their families more than I can ever express in words.

Preface

My story is a little different from others that have been written covering the heyday of BMC Competitions Department/British Leyland Competitions. This book is all about my experiences during the 45 years I worked in the motor industry. It does, of course, include my apprenticeship, the years I spent in the Competitions Department at Abingdon, my time at Citroën and the first five years of my retirement.

Several people have published their own account of working within the BMC/British Leyland Competitions Department, and I apologize in advance if there are any areas that overlap their experiences, or are repeated.

I have gathered information from many sources and I would like to thank all those people who willingly volunteered or who unknowingly gave me information from one source or another. A special thanks to Peter Browning, Stuart Turner, Paddy Hopkirk, Bill Price and Brian Moylan. The books they wrote on the BMC Competitions Department were extremely useful when I was researching information and facts for my own book.

There are several incidents in my story that I am not very proud of, yet the book would not have been complete had I left them out, nor would it have had the same impact without them. I send my heartfelt apologies to anyone who may be upset, hurt or offended by any of the events that have been described in the following chapters.

My good fortune in life, I maintain, has been down to the fact that I have almost always been in the right place at the right time. The one occasion when I was in the wrong place at the wrong time resulted in a night in jail.

Without the persistent badgering and persuasion of a number of close friends, family and former colleagues over the years, it has become apparent that this account of my life would not exist in a physical form. When I finally succumbed and set about putting the story together, however, little did I anticipate all the trials and tribulations that would go along with it.

Writing this book has unlocked doors in my subconscious mind that would otherwise have probably stayed locked forever. Nevertheless, I have to admit that as time went by I really began to enjoy penning my memoirs, and, let's face it, I'll probably never write another book as I can't imagine the next 20 years being as eventful (that's supposing I live another 20 years), or as fulfilling as the first 65.

Contents

My Childhood	1
MG's Before the Apprenticeship	27
The Apprenticeship	34
Apprentice Training School	35
The Production Parts Department	37
Nuts and Bolts Store	38
Good Inwards Inspection	39
Tool Store	39
Tool Room	40
The Press Shop	42
The Production Lines	42
Time and Motion Study	43
Show Department	44
Production Road Test	45
Inspection	46
The Garage	46
The Tyre Bay	47
Rectification	48
Paint Shop	50
Service Department	52
Competitions Department	54
Drawing Office	56
Development Department	58

Planning Office	61
Conducted Tours of the MG Factory	62
The Last Three Months	63
Educational Visits	64
Rag Week	67
Abingdon Polytechnic & Oxford College of Art & Commerce	69
Sports	71
Eskdale Outward Bound Course - 1961	73
Motor Shows	81
British Leyland Apprentices Continental Tour	82
A Lesson to Be Learned	84
The Apprentices' Association	85
Show Department	86
Competitions Department	89
Monte Carlo Rally 1965	92
Alpine Rally	95
Testing in Wales	96
RAC Rally	97
Monte Carlo 1966	100
Tulip Rally	104
Acropolis Experiences	104
Acropolis Rally 1966	105
Alpine Rally	110
The RAC Rally 1966	111
Stuart Turner Resigns	112

Monte Carlo 1967	113
San Remo Rally 1967	117
Stuart's Farewell	119
Tulip Rally 1967	120
Acropolis Rally 1967	122
Austrian Rally School	135
Alpine Rally	136
My first born	138
RAC Rally	138
Monte Carlo Rally 1968	139
East African Safari Rally 1968	141
Tulip Rally 1968	149
A Three-Month Interlude	150
The merger	170
1969 Programme	170
Brands Hatch	171
Silverstone	172
Hockenheim Circuit	173
European Six-Hour Race	175
Mallory Park	175
Spa 24 Hour	176
Tour de France 1969	176
RAC Rally	179
World Cup Rally Experiences London – Mexico 1970	181
Marathon de la Route - Nurburgring	210

The Closure — 214
   Life in the Retail Trade — 215

Citroën UK Ltd. — 236
   Exhibitions — 260

   Fleet Manager — 262

   Corporate Entertaining — 269

   Club Captain — 281

My Retirement — 290
   24 Heures du Mans 2007 — 308

My Childhood

I entered this world in the historic market town of Abingdon in Berkshire (now Oxfordshire) on 16 April 1943. I was the third child of Horace and Helen (Ethel, as I always called her) Pike. Ahead of me were my two older brothers. John, the eldest, was born on 22 February 1938, and Bill (William) on 5 July 1940. I was christened Dudley and, for some reason, I was the only child in the family to have one forename. I believe that my parents had run out of names and imagination, or that I had just caught them by surprise.

Home was an average-sized three-bedroomed semi-detached house in Abingdon's Sellwood Road, and I lived there for some 21 years before moving out just after my 21st birthday. My next home, which I purchased in 1964, was a brand new three-bedroomed house which cost the princely sum of £2,750. It was located in Grove, near Wantage in Berkshire, and I lived there with my first wife, Jean.

One of the earliest memories I have from the very early days of my childhood involves the bad weather of 1947 and the extreme havoc and chaos it caused. The stream, or brook as we called it, at the bottom of the garden flooded into all the nearby gardens, and in the lower places it spilled into the road. The water rose to within an inch off the top of the backdoor step, and I remember Mum, Dad and the neighbours heaving the furniture upstairs so that it wouldn't get damaged. Dad covered all the air bricks below the damp course, but I still think the water got under the house. After rescuing all the furniture from the ground floor and attempting to prevent any more water coming in, all the neighbours, including our family, moved onto the next house and carried out the same exercise there. I think in those days there was much more camaraderie between neighbours and that they were much closer than they are today. For one thing, not many people had televisions or computers and iPods did not exist. People made their own entertainment.

The floods were followed by a big freeze which lasted for several weeks and whilst they salted the roads like they do today, the equipment used in those days was nothing like the modern gritting lorries that most of us are used to seeing these days.

My parents kept a lot of caged rabbits in the garden when we were growing up. Each of us kids had our own favourite which we'd name and keep as our pet. They were housed in 20ft-long cages that were stacked three cages high. Dad would always confuse us by moving them from cage to cage as they grew bigger. However, our dad only kept them in order to breed them for food. The largest rabbits, which would be eaten first, were kept at one end, and the smaller ones at the other. This was done not only to separate the big and small rabbits, which were always fighting, but also to make the ones ready to eat more accessible. Every so often, we'd come home and wouldn't be able to find our adopted pet. If Dad had moved the rabbit, he'd show us its new location. However, when there was a more sinister reason for the rabbit's disappearance, he would come up with the excuse that the rabbit had escaped into the neighbour's garden when he had opened the door of the cage to feed it, and he couldn't find it for all his want of trying. We'd always believe him and would even spend more time looking for our favourite rabbit just in case it was stranded somewhere nearby waiting to be found. Little did we know, though, that the rabbit stew was already simmering on the gas stove.

Although we loved keeping rabbits at home, there was a down side to it. Once or twice a week we had to nip over to the adjacent fields from our house to collect feed for them to eat. We mainly gathered dandelions and cow parsley, as these plants seemed to suit their culinary habits very well. Not only that, but they helped to fatten them up extremely quickly too.

If I think about it, I never once saw Dad slaughter a single rabbit that we ever owned, and, to this day, I believe that he used to take them across the road to a neighbour who would carry out the dastardly deed instead. I do know for a fact that we did eat every single one of them, though, and it was a good job that every member of the family liked rabbit otherwise they would have certainly missed out on their ration of meat.

Apart from the above, the recollection of my early years is a bit hazy. From the age of five I attended the primary school in Conduit Road, Abingdon. The headmistress, who was very old (to a five year old), was called Miss Breed. She was extremely strict and most of the children were petrified of her. Needless to say, we knew her weakness and always managed to find a way of getting round her to our advantage.

When I was seven or eight, I joined the Cub Scouts. The Cub's headquarters were in Sellwood Road and only a three-minute walk from my house. This was a busy age for me, as around the same time I was also a choirboy at the Trinity Methodist Church in Abingdon. Nobody believes me to this day, yet there is a photograph of me standing by the font singing my heart out somewhere, but, alas, I cannot find it to prove my facts.

Builders had started to construct Dunmore County Primary School during this period of my childhood and all this was going on immediately at the rear of our house. We only had to jump the stream at the bottom of the garden to arrive on site and we spent many hours playing there, as did lots of other local children. The builders and the police had a hard time of it and much of their duty was taken up with chasing us away. We were marched home to our parents on numerous occasions by various police officers, who then proceeded to lecture our parents on the dangers of playing on a half-finished building site. Dad, needless to say, was furious, and we often came into contact with the back of his belt as punishment. Despite all of this, we were still undeterred and always found ourselves back on the site the following day.

One of my old next door neighbour's relatives owned a small plot of land in Kempsey, Worcestershire, and every now and again one of us would be invited down there to stay for the weekend. Bill and I seemed to take it in turns. It was always such an adventure down there and so different from our normal home-life routine back in Abingdon. Whilst at home we delighted in caring for our pet rabbits, in Kempsey we revelled in feeding the chickens and ducks and in collecting all their eggs as soon as they had been laid. The geese were not so friendly, however, and often gave chase whilst sounding threateningly angry squawks. We simulated what can only be described as a child – goose version of *hide and seek*, which always ended up in the fowl very quickly discovering our hiding place and us having to run off again. On other occasions, we were instructed to help with milking the cows, but there were so few of them that by the time we got out of bed all the morning milking had been done.

After my stint at Carswell Primary School I progressed up into the junior school, which was also under the supervision of the dreaded Miss Breed. I'm unable to recall many of my young classmates from this time, but there is one who stood out and has stuck in my mind to this day. There was a girl called Pauline, who I thought was the bees' knees, and she was my first ever girlfriend. We always sat together in class and whenever there was a school play, function or Christmas party, this was a reason to arrive home later. What this really meant was more time for us to spend together without it looking suspicious!

I suppose that when I think about it, this was probably about the time when I first started to notice the more attractive qualities in the opposite sex. They were particularly apparent in the older girls, who seemed to take on a very appealing shape that I found extremely pleasing to the eye.

By the time I was due to go to senior school, the school had moved to a new premises in Farringdon Road, Abingdon. It had also changed its name to Larkmead Secondary Modern School.

A new school meant a new attitude. I hated school with a passion, yet I was determined to make the effort to enjoy it and make the most out of the five years that lay ahead. I realized that growing up and going to junior school was a huge experience that would set me up for future years.

We had been installed in the new school for about six months before the official inauguration took place. The ceremony, which was attended by the education minister at the time, was held in the main assembly hall, which was too small to hold all the students and dignitaries that had been invited. This meant that most of the students had the ceremony relayed to them whilst they were sat in their classrooms.

As the minister gave his important speech, I was unfortunately caught talking to my desk mate, and we were both dispatched to the woodwork master for immediate punishment. Punishment involved a homemade table tennis bat with a very long handle that had been manufactured out of plywood. The long handle, in this case, was used as a cane, and despite only receiving three strokes of the bat, it was painful enough for us to regret our decision to talk, or rather talk and get caught. If a teacher even came near you with such an instrument today, they would most likely never teach again.

Going to senior school coincided with me becoming a Boy Scout, which I enjoyed immensely. My parents encouraged me to take part in all the activities available including the weekend camps at the Youlbury Scout Activity Centre located at Boars Hill, just outside of Oxford.

I loved those weekends away camping, especially at the regional or county competition camps that took place every month during the summer period. My competitive nature was already on display, even at such a young age.

Even there, though, I wasn't able to stay out of trouble. When I was slightly older, I was quite partial to a cigarette back then. I remember one day I was running across the camp when I tripped over and fell onto the ground, along with my cigarette packet which had fallen out of my pocket. To my horror, when I stood up, I came face to face with the Scout master, who was menacingly towering above me holding my cigarettes in his hand. Yes, this ended up in another rollicking, which was bad enough, but I didn't even get my cigarettes back either.

The main lessons that I gleaned from being involved with the Scouts' organisation, other than those of preparing me in general for the future, were learning to cook – always good for a man to know how to do – and the art of how to get along with other people. I have made use of both skills all throughout my adult life, and both have been extremely handy to me.

These days of my youth were amongst some of the best moments of my life. It was during my Scouts' time that I was selected on three occasions to perform and take part in the local Gang Show. This was an annual theatrical performance carried out by the youth members of the Scouts. Our Gang Show was held at the Oxford Playhouse Theatre and it ran for a week, although we had to spend weeks beforehand rehearsing. My performances consisted of two stints singing in the chorus, and a third time acting the part of an old woman in a sketch about a public toilet attendant.

What stood out for me was the camaraderie between all the lads from the various groups from all across Oxford. It was admirable and, on reflection, I feel that at this time of my life I was really living life to the full, despite my tender age.

Together with the Scouts and camping, football was my other passion, and I was into it in a big way. At senior school I was playing in the second team by the age of 13, and made it into the first team just a year later. I was also good enough to get selected for the Under 16 Berkshire County Schoolboy's team. We played three games, winning just one and losing two, against some of the teams from nearby counties.

While I loved football and enjoyed everything that it entailed, playing a match against another school did give me the perfect alibi to miss the odd lesson or two, which generally turned out to be a whole afternoon in some cases. This made playing football even more agreeable.

As you may have gathered, I wasn't a great fan of going to school, but it wasn't all bad. In fact, there were a number of teachers who actually made a huge impact on my life, and they stood out (in more ways than one) miles above the rest.

First of all, there was my English teacher. He was fantastic. No matter what the topic of the day was, he would make the lesson so interesting that the whole class would sit in silence, completely enthralled in the subject and hanging off his every word. When the bell sounded to indicate the end of that class, we would all be slightly disappointed. For this reason, I've always loved English, literature and writing.

My maths teacher was another who made a massive impression on me and I can safely say that I looked up to him and admired him a lot. Perhaps if it hadn't been for him, I wouldn't have attained such exceptional results in my maths exams. He was extremely strict, which was probably due to the fact that he was so short and felt that he had to make up for it somehow. He was also quite odd-looking with his dark complexion and pencil-thin moustache. Despite suffering from Little Man Syndrome, he was totally respected by the whole class and made each student feel important as he spent time with each and every one of us making sure that we understood the work we'd been assigned.

Last, but definitely not least, there was the music teacher. Wow, what a woman! I can still picture her in my mind's eye to this day. She was a stunning lady in her late twenties or early thirties, and all the boys in our class were completely infatuated with her, including me. And, it wasn't difficult to understand why as she had the most stunning figure — the most outstanding breasts, and her behind was like two perfectly rounded ostrich eggs. In those days, women seemed to wear different shaped bras, which to me were more pointed that those that women wear today. This just enhanced her assets even more under the tight sweaters she always used to wear. It wasn't just me, but all the young and impressionable 12 and 13-year-old boys in my school took notice of what was in front of them when she was around.

We were all extremely envious of the P.E. master, who seemed to have a very close relationship with her and spent more time with her then he perhaps should have.

Our sports education at school consisted of two lessons a week. During the winter months, one of those lessons, which usually took place on a Friday morning, constituted a cross-country run. I remember these well, not because I enjoyed them, but because they were a real chore for me and I would try anything to get out of them. And, I mean anything.

My friend and I actually decided to devise a plan so that we could get out of the monotonous routine which neither of us liked one bit.

Every two weeks we had to run two circuits of the area. A circuit consisted of running along the road, round the school and returning back to the start via the school sports ground and through the school's own allotments, where our gardening lessons took place. The allotments were fairly isolated and housed a large shed where all the gardening equipment, such as bags of fertiliser, big heavy-duty sacks and lots of utensils, was kept. We decided that the shed was the ideal place to hide due to the fact that we passed it twice during the run. This meant that if we slipped off and hid in the shed the first time round, we could re-join the group on the second leg and make it look like we'd been there all along.

The only problem was that the shed was always kept locked and, naturally, we didn't have a key. Nevertheless, that didn't stop us as I came up with an ingenious idea of how to get one.

At the end of our next gardening lesson, I volunteered to put all the tools away, return them to the shed and lock the door behind me. Fortunately for us, our gardening lesson took place in the period just before lunch and I accidently forgot to return the key and went off on my break. On this occasion I didn't join my pals for lunch, I legged it down to the local hardware store – this time my enthusiasm for running increased immensely – and got a copy of the shed key cut before quickly legging it back. After lunch I returned the original back to the gardening master and apologised profusely. The teacher was not happy at all and gave me a huge dressing down, but it was worth it as we got away with it, and ended up with the key to our problem.

By the time the next cross-country lesson came around, we were ready to put everything into action and see if our plan really would work. We slipped away without anyone noticing and spent most of the lesson quite comfortably ensconced in the shed. As the leaders of the group came into sight for the second time, we got ready to leave. We managed to silently creep back into the group without arousing too much suspicion, although a few boys did ask us what we'd been up to when they saw us emerge from the back of the shed. We told them that we'd just been for a pee and left it at that.

Now, believe it or not, that gardening shed was also extremely instrumental to my introduction to the birds and the bees. A few weeks later, while we were in the shed, we suddenly noticed to our amazement that the P.E. teacher and the music teacher were heading towards us. In a blind panic and with no idea of how we were going to get out of this one, we threw ourselves amongst all the equipment and decided to try and hide, thoroughly expecting all hell to break loose after about 30 seconds. The door opened and they both entered, but what happened next completely stunned me and became the catalyst for a new chapter in my life. While the incident was a total shock and has remained etched onto my brain to this day, it was truly exciting at the same time and I'll never forget the show that they inadvertently put on for us for the rest of my days.

The P.E. teacher undressed her in a very methodical fashion, yet she was the exact opposite, almost ripping his clothes off. They started off with some very intense foreplay, both going down on each other before the actual act of intercourse took place. At the time, I remember thinking it was a bit rough and hard, but then I was obviously completely inexperienced at that age and didn't know any different. There was no doubt in my mind, however, that she was enjoying every minute of it and neither of them seemed in any hurry for it to end. Like her, my friend and I were both also extremely disappointed when their activities did finally come to a climax and finish.

This was my first experience of seeing a naked woman and the music teacher had a stunning body, with breasts that most women would be envious of and which the majority of men would love to handle.

Before we could sneak out from our hiding place we had to wait for the couple to get dressed again. When they were a safe distance away, we snuck out and ran past them as if nothing had happened, just making it back in time by the skin of our teeth and being the last ones to complete the run.

On a completely different note, a few days later as we queued up to enter the gym, the P.E. master asked me if I was chewing gum. Without thinking of the consequences of my impudence, I replied that indeed I was and would he like some. The comment went unpunished, that is until we were all lined up outside in our P.E. kits and the P.E. master called me out to the front of the class. He bent me over and gave me three strokes of his huge table tennis bat, warning the others that the same would happen to anyone else who wanted to be cheeky. The pain was excruciating beyond belief and when he ordered me back to my place, I just carried on walking straight in the direction of the door. In response to him questioning my actions, I replied that I was going home as there was no way I was going to let any teacher abuse me like that. I was obviously growing up.

The next day I was called before the headmaster, who questioned me about the incident. I accused the P.E. teacher of being a sadist who liked to administer torture, not punishment, which could have been said about a few of the others too! I naturally received a dressing down about my behaviour, however, within a few days, both the teachers who administered their own form of punishment with their homemade weapons stopped doing so.

In any case, returning back to the sexual shed incident and my early introduction to the birds and the bees, I reckon that this episode had such an impact that it fired up a natural interest in sex and the female form in me that stayed with me for life.

Around the age of 14, I remember I was very smitten with a girl called Joanne. She left school early every Thursday afternoon to go to a music lesson in town and I always found some excuse to leave early that day too, just so I could walk with her. I managed to steer her off into the park on the way, where we'd stop for a kiss and a cuddle. Joanne was a great girl and we spent a lot of time together inside and outside of school. Sadly, she moved away and we ended up losing contact.

But, it wasn't long before another girl caught my attention. Her name was Irene and she lived in the RAF quarters in Abingdon with her parents, as did many of my school friends. The RAF camp was about five miles from my home and I'd often cycle up to see my friends that lived there. That's how I met Irene.

She was also a lovely girl, but I can't deny that I was first became interested in her because of her attractive features and well-developed body. It wasn't long before I'd ditched my friends and I'd cycle up to Irene's house three times a week instead. From her house we'd both cycle to an isolated spot that we had discovered together, where I delighted in exploring her body and ample curves. We really did enjoy some very sensuous evenings together as well as having lots of fun too.

One of my good friends, Geoff, lived at the Dr Barnardo's home located on the other side of Abingdon. The home, Caldecott House, was a grand, Old Saxon manor house which dated back to 1738. It opened as a Dr Barnardo's home in 1945 and became mixed several years later in 1952. The annual summer fete held at Caldecott House was one of the highlights on the Abingdon calendar, with celebrities such as Princess Margaret, Jack Hawkins and Sir Edmund Hillary often presiding the event.

Anyway, the grounds of Caldecott House were vast and contained sports facilities and an adventure park with rope ladders, slides, swings and so much more to entertain young, adventurous children.

I loved going there to see Geoff and often spent many weekends and time during the school holidays at Caldecott House, or rather in the outside grounds. Walter Brampton, the warden of the home, was always happy to see me and didn't have any problem whatsoever with me being there. Looking back now, though, I wish that I'd asked Geoff and his twin sister Margaret to come home to my house and spend time with me and my family.

At the age of 14 or 15, I took up ballroom dancing and attended the Bretts School of Dancing with my partner, and girlfriend of the time, Yvonne. Yvonne's cousin, Sandra, and her partner, Clifford, used to come along too, and the four of us enjoyed many a Saturday morning learning how to dance.

After some time, we left Bretts and joined a dance club at Northcourt Hall, where lessons took place every Tuesday evening. In those days, we didn't get homework from school, so a late night with an early morning rise the following day didn't worry us. We persevered for about three years and managed to gain a bronze and a couple of silver medals, namely in the Quick Step, Foxtrot, Tango and the Waltz.

Yvonne and I met through our mums, as they both worked together in the Dunmore Country Primary School kitchens. I eventually lost contact with Yvonne due to having different interests as we got older. However, I was delighted when she contacted me a few years ago through Friends Reunited and offered me some much needed information on the dancing sessions we used to enjoy together.

I was also quite musical in my younger years and during my time at the Scouts, I formed a skiffle group with four of my friends. There were two of us on guitar, one on drums, a bass player (tea chest and broomstick) and the last member was on the washboard with thimbles. Our idol at that time was Lonnie Donegan and we performed his music at all the

Scout functions as well as in all the places that would have us. Fortunately for our neighbours, we were given permission to practise in the Scout hall when it wasn't in use. The acoustics were appalling, but at least there weren't any complaints from any angry residents.

My brother John was seven years older than me and was called up for National Service. He opted to join the Royal Marines Commandos and spent time away in Plymouth, Malta and Cyprus. I remember I used to look forward to his return home as he'd always take me to the cinema in Oxford as a special treat.

Bill, my middle brother, like me, escaped National Service, although I believe that Bill had to get a deferment as he was about two years into his apprenticeship at the time of call up.

I didn't have a particularly privileged childhood. Mum and Dad were never very well-off due to the fact that during his thirties Dad suffered with osteomyelitis, which resulted in him spending several years at the Nuffield Orthopaedic Hospital in Oxford. Mum had to contend with raising three boys with seven years between us – a tough job considering that we didn't make it very easy for her. If I say that we were extremely well-behaved and innocent, you'd do well not to believe a word of it.

Unfortunately, as a result of Dad's long illness he lost his job at MG's. Nevertheless, thanks to the kindness and compassion of John Thornley, the managing director of the company at the time, he was given an administrative position in production control as soon as he was fit enough to return to work again.

My father had previously worked on the manual side of things, but after his illness he could only take on an administrative role, which paid less. However, as far back as I can remember, I cannot recall that us kids ever went without when we were young. Our parents did a superb job in bringing us up. It may not have been without its troubles, though, which is probably what turned my father's hair grey. Not to worry, though, he made sure that I inherited every single one of those grey hairs back.

Our grandparents lived in Egham, in Surrey, and they were members of the Plymouth Brethren Christian Church, an extremely strict religious sect. When we used to visit, the only things that we were allowed to do were play Draughts, Snakes and Ladders or do puzzles. These were the only forms of entertainment that were permitted by their religion. Forget watching television, drinking alcohol or playing any card game whatsoever. They were all banned. Even the card game Snap was considered to be a form of gambling by my grandfather.

Nevertheless, I like to think that there's a positive to every story, and, in this case, I actually became quite an expert at playing Draughts. This is great as it frustrates the life out of my grandchildren, who mistakenly thought that their granddad would be a pushover in this game. They haven't yet beaten me to this day, although every time that we do play together I have noticed their improvement each time. It won't be long before they finally get one over on me.

Keeping rabbits has somewhat been a tradition in my family as my grandfather used to breed them too, although he had twice as many as we used to at home. When he slaughtered them, he used to let them hang for a couple of days to improve the flavour, he said.

During one visit to our grandparents' house, I remember seeing a rabbit hanging in the kitchen and was convinced that it had moved. I continued to stare at this dead rabbit and, sure enough, my eyes hadn't been deceiving me as I saw it move for a second time. I mentioned this to my grandmother and she suggested that as the animal had been hanging there for a few days, maybe it had a couple of "guests" inside. It became totally apparent what she meant by "guests" when Granddad cut the rabbit open that night to clean it, and it was crawling full of maggots.

The flavour, however, was one that you could only associate with game, not an unpleasant flavour, but one that I still cannot describe to this day.

My Plymouth Brethren grandparents belonged to my mother's side. She had had to put up with an austere upbringing since the day she was born and by the time she reached the age of 18, she knew that she'd had enough and decided to leave her home, and the Christian Church, forever. Much to the disappointment and frustration of her parents and indeed some of her other relatives, she packed her bags and went off to work in service. During her career she worked in some of the biggest houses in London, Oxford and Woodstock.

Mum and Dad met in Oxford when Mum went to work for Dad's sister, Auntie Phil, or Nurse Pike as she was commonly known in the area. Auntie Phil, who worked as a midwife, lived in James Street in Cowley, Oxford, where she used her home as a maternity home for young mothers. These young girls would come to her house to give birth then stay with her for a few days until they were ready to take their baby and return to their own home.

Mum helped out generally in the maternity home and some of her tasks involved nursing both mother and baby during their stay. While Mum was working with Auntie Phil, Dad was living with her, and this is how our parents met. On occasions, they even helped treat some of Nurse Pike's patients together.

Before moving in with Auntie Phil, Mum looked after an elderly lady in Woodstock, near Oxford. The woman was extremely well-off, but she had a terrible drink problem. When we were little, Mum always used to regale us with the story about when the lady would run out of gin and couldn't get hold of any other form of alcohol, she would drink eau de Cologne instead. She always had a supply of it as she had it delivered to the house in pint-sized bottles.

Mum had three brothers – Charles, Vernon and Peter – and she was the third child out of the four. All three of her brothers worked for a short time at the tailor's that their father used to work in until they all found their feet and went on to do other things.

When Charles got married, the couple immigrated to

Australia and adopted a boy, Colin, who became my cousin. Vernon married a German lady – which caused them a load of problems during the war years – and they went on to have three children; my other cousins, Stuart, Jennifer and Nigel.

Peter, who married Vera, was in the RAF. They didn't go on to have any children or provide me with any more cousins from my mother's side. Peter, sadly passed away in 1982 unexpectedly. He was travelling up North and suffered a bleed to his stomach. He was rushed to hospital and spent three weeks in intensive care in a hospital in Birmingham, but during the third week, he gave up the strength to live and passed away in his sleep. Peter was a lovely man and he and I got on very well right up until the day he died.

My father came from a slightly larger family. He was one of six children. There were two brothers, one of who died from cancer in his twenties, and four sisters: Dorothy, Ruby, Phyllis and Amy.

As far as I know, my Auntie Amy met her husband in Oxford while he was studying to become a lawyer. After they married they moved to India and lived on a tea plantation. They enjoyed a very comfortable life as her husband either part-owned the plantation or just managed it. Either way, they were extremely well-off. That was until Aunt Amy's husband died, however, in 1970. Upon his death, she returned to England a very frail lady and went to live with Auntie Phil. Despite the love and care she received from Auntie Phil, Amy passed away at the beginning of the following year. This was such a shame because none of the family really had the opportunity to get to know her that well.

The others remained in Oxford for most of their lives except for Auntie Ruby. Auntie Ruby and her husband, Arthur, had two children, David and Gill, but when her husband died, Auntie Ruby headed off for New Zealand with her daughter and grandson in 1975. Ruby's son, David, remained in the village of Cumnor, near Oxford.

I remember one Sunday afternoon I decided to take a ride to visit my Auntie and Uncle who were living at the time around 30 miles away. When I arrived, I noted that whilst obviously pleased to see me, there was a slight hint of tension and uneasiness at the same time. It wasn't long before I found out why as, my cousin, suddenly appeared fostering a huge belly. She was eight months pregnant, unmarried, still living at home with her parents and they'd all kept this little secret from the rest of the family – up until my visit to them, that is. It was hardly surprising, though, as there was still quite a stigma attached to being unmarried and with child in 1958.

To say that I was slightly shocked was a bit of an understatement, but I had seen her with my own eyes and knew it to be true. When I got home and told my parents, however, my mother didn't believe a single word I was telling her. At that time we didn't have a telephone, but I'm sure that that night my mother walked down to the nearest telephone box at the end of the road and called them to find out whether there actually was any truth to the matter.

We never did find out who the baby's father was but I do know that he did not have much to do with my second cousin. However it did not do him any harm as he turn out to be a super person and I believe he is now living in the north of England with his wife and family.

One of my dad's other sisters, Dorothy, married a guy called Bill Street, who worked as a solicitor's clerk. Their daughter, Jean, moved to the Costa del Sol in 1995. Dorothy and Bill, on the other hand, lived just outside Oxford's city centre all their married life until Bill passed away in the early seventies. After her husband's death, Dorothy moved to Bedford to be closer to her daughter before she moved to Spain.

Mum and Dad got married at the Saint Mary and Saint John Church in Cowley St John, Oxford, on 21 December 1935. While they waited for their marital home to be completed they lived in a flat in Bath Street in Abingdon with an old lady called Miss Faulkner.

The old lady was always busy either in the garden or in the kitchen and you could usually guess what she'd been up to from the stains on her hands and clothes.

Despite the fact that they lived in a flat, Miss Faulkner's home had a huge garden attached to it that was full of fruit trees. During the season, she'd provide Mum with an endless supply of fruit.

Later on, after Mum and Dad moved into their own home in 1940-1, they would still take us to see Miss Faulkner because her house was situated on the corner of Bath Street and Park Road, and almost in the centre. Miss Faulkner used to let us leave our bikes at her house until we came back from town.

If any of us boys were in town with our mates, we'd make sure we popped in because she always handed us a carrier bag full of apples, pears or plums if we asked.

Mum and Dad's new house was in Sellwood Road, Abingdon, and it cost them the princely sum of £700. We all lived there until a few years after my father's death on 24 October 1964. The large garden, which would be considered huge in today's standards, just became too much for Mum, and so she decided to downsize to a two-bedroomed bungalow in Portway, Didcot, in Berkshire. The new house also had a large garden, but it was a quarter of the size of the Sellwood Road one. Unfortunately, it also turned out to become a burden for her.

I did offer her some help with the garden, though. It was around this time that I bought a Rotovator with my second wife's father, who also had a big garden, and every February or early March I'd go over to Mum's with the Rotovator to work the whole garden for her. Once this had been done she was able to plant a lovely selection of her favourite vegetables. Whenever we went to visit, she'd always give us a guided tour of the garden, pointing out which plants were thriving and growing well.

Mother stayed at the bungalow in Didcot until she moved in with Bill and Margaret while she was waiting to get a warden-controlled apartment in Lady Eleanor Court. This retirement home was run by Anchor, the largest not-for-profit provider of housing and care for the over 55s in England. Mum was desperate to get into one of these retirement properties, but Anchor would not put her on the priority list while she still owned her own home in Didcot. To solve the matter Mum sold up and moved in with my brother.

Not surprisingly, within a few months Mum's name had quickly moved up on the waiting list and it wasn't long before she was awarded a lovely little one-bedroom apartment in Lady Eleanor Court in Abingdon, like she wanted.

Mum had a fantastic time living in Eleanor Court and she made a lot of new friends there. She was even voted Deputy Warden at the age of 80 – a post which she held for about two years.

While Mum was living in Eleanor Court, the emergency system was changed and updated. The new system meant that when anyone pulled the emergency cord a call centre in Manchester would be alerted. Poor Mum, bless her, could never get her head round this as she couldn't work out how someone in Manchester could help them in Abingdon. She obviously didn't realise that up in Manchester they'd just press the right buttons and local Abingdon emergency services would leap into action and come to the rescue.

When my mother was 90 years old she was unexpectedly diagnosed as having breast cancer. She underwent a mastectomy, which was carried out at the Churchill hospital in Oxford, and recovered from the whole ordeal remarkably well for someone of her age. After a bout of radiotherapy she was given the all clear, despite being left with a nasty rash that itched like mad caused from damaged skin.

Mum unfortunately had to leave Lady Eleanor when she had a fall and suffered a broken hip at the age of 91. She was treated at the John Ratcliffe Hospital in Oxford where they operated and inserted a pin in her thigh and hip. This situation meant that her mobility was totally hindered and therefore she wasn't allowed to return home. After six days at the hospital Mum was transferred to the Marcham Road Hospital, a small cottage hospital on the outskirts of Abingdon, and from there to a nursing home in Wallingford that my brothers found when it was evident that she needed full-time care. Mum stayed in the new place for about three years until she suffered another fall.

This was around the time that I'd been offered a job in Spain. I didn't know what to do as I felt guilty for leaving Mum, but we had a long chat and she said that she was more than happy for us to go. So, that was it; we moved to Spain lock, stock and barrel. My brothers and sisters-in-law weren't so over the moon as we were, though, and accused me of abandoning Mum and not caring about her. It did actually cause quite a rift in the family, which will be explained in more detail in the chapter on retirement later in the book.

MG's Before the Apprenticeship

In my last year of school I used to cycle to Marcham with a friend whose uncle also had small holding and we used to help them by mucking out the milking parlour and harvesting the turnips and a root vegetable which they called a mango and storing them for the winter as a lot of them were used for cattle feed. I always seemed to be attracted to animals and have very little fear of them regardless of size; which means that they can take you by surprise and sometimes catch you out.

I left school in April 1958 and started my employment with the MG Car Company straightaway. In those days if your fifteenth birthday fell before or during the Easter holidays, then you were permitted to leave school at the end of that term providing you had a job to go to. This is exactly what I did, much to the envy of many of my friends who were unable to leave until July.

Back then, it was practically impossible to get into Gee's unless you had some family connection to someone who already worked there. I was very fortunate as my father and my two brothers had already been installed there for some time when it was my turn to look for a job. What made it even easier for me than for most was that Dad was very much respected within the company, and so us boys going to work there was never really in doubt.

My first six months at the Gee's were spent working in the Goods Inwards department, which, on reflection, was an extremely good grounding into the company. My tasks consisted of delivering the goods that arrived at the company from outside to every department within the factory. Apart from familiarizing myself with the whole layout and set-up, I also got to know everyone that worked there. My colleagues taught me a lot of life skills that would be useful to me later on, such as all about horse racing, snuff and how to make a job last longer than it really should.

After my initial six months at Goods Inwards I was moved to the MG trim line, where I learnt all about working on the production lines. Here, I also picked up very handy extra-curricular information that would keep me in good stead later on in life. It wasn't long before I worked out that if I helped the operators with their sub-assemblies, they would most likely tip me somewhere in the region of 50p to a pound for my trouble. While this doesn't seem like a lot of money, bear in mind that my weekly wage back in 1958 was only £3.20 a week. Add to this the fact that as I was looking after around 20 blokes, all the 50ps and one pounds amounted to quite a considerable sum. With the tips that I collected here, I was able to pay for certain luxuries like playing darts, billiards and alcohol – all very valuable when growing up and wanting to become streetwise.

I spent just three months in the MG trim line department before I was transferred to the MGB assembly line, where once again I quickly worked out which employees were generous with their tips and dedicated more of my time to helping them. As well as keeping an eye on my money and extra income sources, there were also a couple of tasty young ladies that caught my eye too.

Although I spent part of my tips on pub activities and

enjoying myself, I did manage to save quite a bit. I'd been working for several months and decided to buy a new racing bike with some of the money that I'd put by. The bike turned out to be quite an ingenious tool for interacting with the opposite sex.

My Aunt Vera and Uncle Peter used to live in a very large house which had three bedrooms, two bathrooms, a spacious lounge, a huge kitchen and dining room and a roomy apartment contained within it. It was located in Horely, near Gatwick, and my pal and I would cycle down to visit every so often.

Despite the hard slog of the 80-mile journey, which took us through Henley, Guildford, the outskirts of Dorking, and Reigate and would last all day, each visit was worth it when we got there.

My aunt was the manager of the typing pool at a large electronics company in Gatwick and so whenever we decided to cycle down to visit, she not only supplied us with accommodation in the apartment, but she set us up with a couple of the girls from her typing pool each time as well.

My grandparents also lived at the big house then. I remember one bank holiday after my grandfather had passed away we decided to go down and stay. My aunt and uncle were off gallivanting elsewhere but they were quite happy for us to go down anyway as we would be company for Grandma, who was left on her own. While we loved to spend time with Grandma, we were also keen to spend time with some younger members of the opposite sex and so arranged to meet the same girls that we'd met the previous time as Vera wasn't about to line up some new ones.

The weather was appalling, and due to the fact that we were both a bit skint, we decided to smuggle the girls up to our room whilst Grandma was having her afternoon 'forty winks'.

Well, time flew, as it does when you're having fun, and it seemed like we'd only been in our room for ten minutes before Grandma had woken up and was knocking at the door wanting my help with something. I shouted out that I was in a state of undress, which was partly true as we were all in a state of undress at that moment, and that I'd come out and help her in a minute or two. After that, clothes went flying and there was a massive panic to get dressed – quietly. As soon as the girls were ready to leave, which wasn't very long after, I distracted Grandma by keeping her talking, while Mike led the girls downstairs and ushered them out of the front door.

Despite all the commotion from the afternoon it didn't put the girls off, and they were delighted to meet up with us later on that night. However, when we suggested all going back to Aunt Vera's house together to continue with where we had left off earlier, that was a different kettle of fish altogether. It's not that they didn't want to get cosy with us again, they were petrified of being caught by my nan.

Fortunately for us we had a back-up plan and it involved the local football ground, which housed a small but very private sheltered area behind the grandstand. We made quite a lot of use out of it over the coming months.

About a year or so later, Mike and I met two girls the same age as us who were from Derby. Us lads were just about to pop into our local, the Spread Eagle pub, on the Northcourt Road in Abingdon when we spotted these two lovely, young girls struggling down the road with some heavy suitcases. Being the young gentlemen that we were, we offered to carry their cases for them – in exchange for a date the following night. They accepted.

We went back to the pub after we'd helped the girls and enjoyed an even better night than usual, probably in anticipation of what was to come the following night.

Despite the fact that we were underage, the landlord of the Spread Eagle never objected to us being there. Mind you, that was probably because we never ever bought any alcoholic drinks, not that he would have served us anyway. What he didn't realize, though, was that everyone else bought us alcoholic drinks every time we won a game of darts.

The night that we had arranged to meet the girls with the cases, without their cases, was a Saturday, and my parents were going out for the evening. We all decided to go back to my house and play some records before my parents left for their night out. The second that the door closed behind them, all our thoughts about playing records had gone out the front door with them.

The girl that I was with had quite a curvy body, if I

remember rightly, and I definitely wanted to explore what was underneath her clothes. I casually flicked the catch of her bra with one hand and it made quite a loud noise as it twanged back. This made us all snigger as it was plainly obvious to everyone what I'd just done. Nevertheless, I still got to feel her breasts and remember to this day how smooth, soft and warm they felt. It wasn't even as if I had a lot to compare them to at that young age.

On Monday morning, Mum returned home from work and informed me that the two girls Mike and I had entertained on Saturday night were the nieces of a woman that she worked with at Dunmore School. Needless to say, from that point on we were careful what we divulged to her as we knew that Mum and her friend also compared notes on what they thought we had been up to.

My relationship with the curvy girl continued even though she lived in Derby, and we used to write to each other in between her coming down to Abingdon to stay with her aunt. One night when she was down visiting it was pouring with rain, but we managed to find a dry spot in the tennis pavilion in the Albert Park. While we carried out our favourite pastime of exploring each other's bodies, we heard the squelching of someone's feet on the wet ground and immediately froze as we thought someone was very close by. We had a good look round but couldn't see anyone as it was so dark, so we carried on. However, after a few minutes we heard the same noises again and guessed that some pervert was spying on us. Feeling slightly uneasy and very disappointed, we grudgingly got up and walked back to her auntie's house for coffee instead. Thinking about it now,

I'm not sure that I remember her putting her knickers back on.

The Apprenticeship

About four years before I started working at the Gee's they introduced a five-year apprenticeship scheme through which young lads were taken on and trained up in all areas of the factory and fabrication line. During the scheme's initial year, only one apprentice was signed up, but this was increased to four a year from the following year.

Unbeknown to me, my father put my name down for the apprenticeship when I was about 13. Even though I was already working at the Gee's it still came as a complete shock when the personnel officer came up to me and asked me if I was still interested. Of course I didn't have to be asked twice and as soon as I relayed my consent I was told to report to the apprentice school the following Monday morning.

Over the course of the five years, each apprentice spent a designated amount of time in the departments listed below. The time varied depending on the complexity of the work carried out in that department. For instance, in a very technical section you would spend six months, whilst in a non-technical one you would only spend one month.

The Apprentice School (Machine Shop)
The Production Parts Department
Nuts and Bolts Store
Good Inwards Inspection
Tool Stores

Tool Room
Press Shop
Production Lines
Time and Motion Study
Show Department
Production Road Test
Inspection Department
The Garage
Tyre Bay
Rectification Department (Production)
Paint Shop
Service Department
Competitions Department
Development Department
Drawing Office
Planning Office

Apprentice Training School

The first six months of the apprenticeship were always spent in the Apprentice Training School. The apprentice would always return to this department for another six months of training after successfully completing the first 18 months. The second visit was much more complicated and the tasks were extremely technical and intricate.

The first task that we were given by the apprentice master during our initial visit was to file a metal block. The aim of this was to end up with two faces at right angles to each other that had to be perfectly square. A couple of the lads would always try and take a shortcut and they'd take the block and grind it on a surface grinder and then file all the grinding marks away afterwards. The canny apprentice master didn't say anything but he would always hand them another block asking them if they could do the same but with a file instead of the surface grinder. I often wondered if the guys that worked in the machine shop, which is where the surface grinder was kept, reported back to the apprentice master, telling him who had used the machine. If done properly, this task would take a week to complete and there weren't any shortcuts.

During our second six-month stint, the apprentice master set up some fairly difficult tasks. Some of these consisted of making different tools that had to be exact, precise and perfect in every way.

For instance, we had to fabricate a scribing block capable of holding a scriber that could scribe a line in any situation onto metal. For this task we had to get to grips with a milling machine, lathe and various types of grinders, amongst other machines and instruments required. After this, we then had to manufacture two identical G-clamps, a Vblock, a clamp and pair of vice grips. If the master was not satisfied with the end result of our labour, he would make us do them again.

This schooling taught me a lot of disciplines as well as how to manage numerous amounts of different machines and tools. One of the most valuable lessons that I took away with me during my time at the Apprentice School was that it is essential to treat each and every machine with great respect, not only because the machine would repay me by working properly, but also because if not operated correctly and sensibly, it could be extremely dangerous.

Whilst my time at the Apprentice School was very informative and great fun, the worst part of it was that the apprentice master was a huge cricket fan. This meant that we had to endure listening to every single lengthy test match on the radio whenever he was around. Portable televisions were not very common in those days, which is probably just as well! As soon as the master left us alone while he attended a meeting, we'd switch channels so we could listen to some decent pop music instead.

The Production Parts Department

The next step was the main parts department. This area was responsible for feeding all of the production lines. Each employee was allocated to a certain area and it was his job to ensure that the fitters never ran out of the parts that they required to do their job. This was a hard task as here you'd find three assembly lines where the body shells were trimmed and another four where the cars were assembled. We often had to do the rounds of our area with a big trolley or pallet trolley in tow as we frequently had to deal with very large parts that were delivered on a stacker truck.

I had a lot of fun working in the production parts department, yet turning up for work every day was also extremely perilous. The guys were great, but many of them boasted a large repertoire of practical jokes that they had no qualms in playing on you or their colleagues. Health and

Safety, as we know it today, was non-existent, which is probably just as well as many of my colleagues would probably have lost their job carrying on the way they did back then.

A common prank that we had to watch out for involved tall hangers and our coats. We used to hang our jackets and coats on a special coat hanger made in the tool shop. The hanger had an extremely long handle, which we used to hook over the heating pipes that stood about five feet above our heads. If you didn't subconsciously keep one eye on your coat at all times, someone would fill the pockets with heavy objects while you weren't looking or were out of the room. Subsequently, as you lifted your coat off the hanger it would come crashing down with the additional weight from the pockets. Anyone who wasn't prepared or quick enough could have got seriously injured. Most of us were always careful every time we went for our coats.

Nuts and Bolts Store

At the time, the Nuts and Bolts Store was a complete and utter nightmare for us apprentices. We couldn't understand the technical value of spending a month of our training in this department. But now, as I look back, I can see that the time here was invaluable as it enabled me to identify the size and character of every single nut, bolt and washer there is simply by looking at it. Being able to recognize a UNF, Whitworth or Gas thread at a glance proved to be a tremendous benefit later on in my career, and spending a month in the Nuts and Bolts Store was not the total waste of time that we had all predicted.

Good Inwards Inspection

Now, this was a fairly tedious department to spend two whole months in. Here, when a part was delivered to us we had to check and confirm that it had been fabricated to the correct specifications by comparing it to its equivalent technical drawing. We usually just inspected a sample percentage, which was generally 10%. However, if any discrepancies were uncovered, it was then necessary to examine the complete delivery. Some items required a more thorough inspection than others depending on their role in the assembled vehicle, yet it was not always possible to carry out the check there and then if you couldn't tell whether the specifications had been met until it had been fitted to the car. Taxing stuff! Nevertheless, the parts that were manufactured by companies within the group were always built to the correct specification and therefore usually sent directly to the productions stores, or even straight to the production line. This was generally the case for engines, gearboxes and axles.

Tool Store

The Tool Store was a very small storeroom which housed every conceivable tool ever made on the planet! As an apprentice, we'd spend one month in this department. That may seem like a long time, but what you have to bear in mind is that MG's was not a modern factory. For instance, its production lines were not automated, and so each operator had to push the car to the next stage of completion. In actual fact, not a lot had changed since the tanks were produced on the same production lines during World War II. Additionally, a lot of the bits and parts we used were actually manufactured by specialist individual employees who worked in various different departments. Most of these individuals seemed to have worked for the company for an entirety.

On a more happy note, I remember one of the most-used practical jokes for new apprentices was to be sent along to the Tool Store for a 'long weight' (long wait), which I think we were all caught out with at least once during our early months of the apprenticeship.

Tool Room

This department was a lot more interesting than the previous one and we got to spend six very interesting months here. At the Tool Room we were taught how to make precision tools – a very intricate and technical task. The tools that we made were destined for the Press Shop and would replace old ones that were worn out or damaged. A mistake here could cost the company a lot of money and time wasted on the production line, which was not appreciated in the slightest.

Despite the fact that many of the men that worked here permanently were admired and respected for their skill and ability and often worked under pressure due to time constraints set by the production, they would never begrudge spending time with an apprentice and teaching him some of what they knew.

Although their job predominantly called for seriousness at all times, the men also had a huge sense of humour and their own supply of practical jokes.

Another prank that involved our outer garments was not so much dangerous as annoying, especially in winter. They would hoist your coat up into the roof using a crane and leave it there. At the end of the day, you'd go to collect it, realize it wasn't where you left it, but you couldn't do anything about it as all the power had been switched off and the person with the keys had left for the day. This meant making your way home without a coat and not being able to retrieve it until the next morning.

There was another trick they used to play on us there that was dangerous – if you weren't prepared. Someone would heat up aluminium, which doesn't change colour when hot, and ask you later to pass it to them. We eventually learnt that if anyone asked you to pass them a piece of metal, we shouldn't do so unless we had spat on in first, just to establish its condition – cold, or hot enough to burn your hand.

We all enjoyed our time in the Tool Room and would have liked to have spent six months there rather than the three that were allocated to us.

The Press Shop

From the Tool Room where we made the precision tools we then moved on to spend two months in the Press Shop. Here, we would set up the presses with the tools that we'd just been working with in the previous department, so it was interesting to see the progression in the cycle.

The Press Shop was an exceptionally busy place. If the press was down and not working, the guys working on it would be on our case to get it up and running again as quickly as possible because an out-of-order press meant that they weren't earning any money.

The Press Room was also incredibly noisy from the din created from the presses punching out all the various components all day long. The majority of operators had problems with their hearing and although I only spent two months in this department, I often wonder whether it was the cause of my deafness today.

The Production Lines

We spent six or seven months on the production lines and my time here enabled me to get to grips with the process of assembling a car. This was of huge benefit to me later on in life as I intrinsically knew which components to remove in order to get to the one that I wanted to work on.

Here, as soon as the daily quota had been reached the employees were allowed to finish and go home, unless you were an apprentice or tea boy, that is, who all had to stay until finishing time. We made use of this extra time by making sub-assemblies for the operators, who would subsequently reward you for your time and effort at the end of the week. Naturally, I made it my business to know which of them paid the most and which would just take advantage of you.

Spending such a long period of time in this one department meant that I got to know the employees better than those in other departments. I actually made some really good friends here, many of whom I'm still in contact with today.

Time and Motion Study

There were only two guys that worked in this department and, unsurprisingly, they were the two most disliked employees within the factory, basically due to the nature of their job.

They had to oversee all the production and how long it took everyone to complete their task. Originally, each function within the production procedure had been timed to see how long it should take to do correctly, and it was the job of these two guys to make sure that everyone stuck to that time. There was a bit of leeway given and time added on for comfort breaks, but that was it.

As you can imagine, working on a production line can be tedious and boring, and you would need to take breaks in order to maintain your focus and concentration. Therefore, it wasn't surprising that all the production workers wanted more time to complete their tasks. The Time and Motion Study guys were not prepared to give it, though, and this often resulted in some very heated discussions and arguments.

As an apprentice, I spent a month in this department, but it was actually really interesting to understand and listen to all the arguments for more or less time put forward from both sides.

Show Department

The Show Department was responsible for looking after all the company demonstrators that were loaned to journalists or dealers who wanted the vehicles for various events or exhibitions.

This was a fairly exciting place to be in the run up to a motor show, more so when not much was happening in that respect. Despite the fact that the Show Department was only small in comparison to the majority of the others, it held an important position in the company and played a major role.

If a car was being lent out, we'd have to check it over beforehand and prepare it if its destination was a major showcasing event.

The most important exhibition that we were involved with was the Earl's Court Motor Show, which was always held in

October. After many years, this event was moved to Birmingham's National Exhibition Centre.

Production Road Test

Being part of the Production Road Testing team was quite a cushy and relaxing number, which made a change from the stress experienced in some of the others. All we had to do during our one month in this section was sit alongside the road tester and listen to his comments.

Back in the day, every single car was actually road tested by an experienced team of testers and drivers who took the cars out on a six-mile journey.

During the road test, if any faults were discovered, they would be recorded onto a card particular for that vehicle. Back at the factory, the car would be sent to the Rectification Department where the imperfections would be corrected.

One of the most common defects was a noisy final drive, which would result in the whole axle being replaced.

The testers were a lively bunch of lads, but there was one that stood out for his immense skill as a driver. His name was Eddie Burnell and his driving ability shone out above the rest. In fact, Eddie ended up as chief road tester for Special Tuning and became the number one test driver for any track testing that the Competitions Department or the company were involved in.

Inspection

The cars being assembled were required to undergo several checks during the construction process. They were given the once over in the Inspection Department once during the middle of the line and also at the end of the trim line before joining the main assembly line. During its time on the main assembly line there were further inspections too, and the Road Test section and the Rectification Department were also classed as part of the inspection procedure. All in all, each vehicle passed through the Inspection Department about eight times during its build life.

Once the car had been put together, all the paintwork was inspected by the team working in the Paint Shop. If the bodywork showed up any defects under the bright lights it was subject to, they would be rectified by the Paint Shop before undergoing a follow-up inspection.

I spent a month in this department, but as I can't remember that much about it, it couldn't have been that enthralling.

The Garage

This section commanded a four-month period during my apprenticeship as it was responsible for looking after every single vehicle that belonged to the company. This included all their cars, fork-lift trucks or car transporters.

The team consisted of about ten people and included a company chauffeur. Every Monday, the chauffeur drove me and the other three apprentices to the Oxford College of Art and Commerce (now Brooks University) and collected us at 5 p.m. when the session there had finished.

Norman, another one noted for his practical jokes, was the foreman of The Garage and a very likeable fellow who we all enjoyed working under. The first job that he delegated to me was to strip and rebuild the engine on a Lister Flatbed, which was used to carry heavy drums of chemicals from the paint storeroom to the Paint Shop. The engine was a two-cylinder, four-stroke petrol engine with a magneto and a magnificent piece of equipment. I set to work and successfully rebuilt the engine, much to the surprise of my colleagues as, apparently, I was the first person to complete such a task without help from anyone else. I expect that in this day and age, as we are talking about machinery used 40 years ago, that not many people have even heard of a Lister Flatbed let alone seen one, and I feel privileged to have worked on such a beast.

The Tyre Bay

We spent one month in this department during which time all we had to learn was which wheels went with which tyre – nothing too strenuous or technical on the brain. Then we had to ensure that we fit the correct type in accordance with the production schedules.

It was a very busy section, as you can imagine. Production was about 1,500 cars per week, and each vehicle had to be fitted with five tyres. That meant that 7,500 wheels and tyres had to be fitted by hand every week by the three guys that were employed by this department. The three guys did an amazing job, though, despite looking like quite an odd trio. One guy was short and stocky, the second was about six foot two and muscular, while the third was very tall but also extremely thin. None of that mattered, however, as they had no problems whatsoever in keeping up with production.

Fitting a wheel and tyre was quite a strenuous job and I'm sure that technology today has modernised the procedure. We had to deal with a heavy-duty stand with a quick-release clamp mechanism which could be adapted to both a steel wheel and a wire one. The wheel was clamped onto the stand and a lubricating fluid applied on to the tyre. Then with a couple of tyre levers, we would position the tyres onto the rim. If the tyres did not easily inflate, we would have to secure a webbing strap around the circumference of the tubeless tyre and then try and inflate them. The webbing strap acted as a seal on the rim of the wheel and made inflating the tyre possible. Back in those days, in the sixties, we only fit wire wheels with tubed tyres, and I suspect that things have changed today and you can also fit them onto wire wheels as well.

Rectification

The work carried out in the Rectification Department was quite complex, which is why we spent six months of our training in it. All of the problems and adjustments required, which the Road Test and Inspection Departments had noted along the way, were handled by the Rectification Department.

Sometimes a car wouldn't start when it reached the end of the production line, or a component did not function or was had been damaged during assembly. This was all sorted out by the guys in Rectification. In many cases, only a simple adjustment had to be made to get the vehicle in top working condition, but in other cases it may be necessary to replace a power unit, gearbox or final drive.
I recall one occasion during my training in the Rectification Department when me and a few others were required to replace about 30 MGB of wiring harnesses as a faulty batch had slipped through Inspection. The task was extremely repetitive, but I quickly memorised the location of all the electrical components, the colour coding of all the wires and the fastest way to change a harness – all good experience in my book! When we carried out a task, it was checked by one of the guys in the department, who would then put his signature to your work before passing it to the Inspection Department. What made changing an engine more interesting was the fact that a pal of mine and I would have a bet to see who could change one the quickest. By the end of the week it was more or less even between us, as one kind of hitch or another would always arise, allowing the other to make headway and win.

Everyone worked at speed on the production line and so it wasn't uncommon for small mistakes to be made or glitches to occur that would hamper your work rate. One of the most common was for nuts and bolts to cross thread, which meant that we had to spend time re-tapping them and replacing them with new ones. Another common problem involved stiff choke or throttle cables, which also required replacing them with new ones in order to bring the product up to the acceptable standard. And bulbs! I can't even begin to estimate how many bulbs in sidelights, headlights and panel lights we had to change. In this case, we not only had to think of the product, but also of the legal requirements of the Vehicle Construction and Use Act.

All in all, my time spent in the Rectification Department was very interesting and enjoyable, and once again, the guys there were a great bunch of people.

Paint Shop

There was never much paint work to be carried out on the cars as little damage was incurred on the production line and what there was, was repaired on a flow line. It was the smaller body components that required some paintwork attention. Items such as the fuel filler cap or tail light plinths were painted in a separate department, the Paint Shop, which was equipped with the proper extraction and ovens necessary for the paint to dry rapidly so that it hardened correctly and could be handled by an operator without damage.

A lot of time was spent polishing on the flow lines, but there were also some very skilled panel beaters who would beat out the odd damaged part on a panel without ruining the paintwork at all. With the aid of a highly polished hammer and dolly, a perfect result was always achieved. This is considered a serious skilful task as these days the average panel beater would find it impossible to hammer out a dent and not have to repaint it afterwards. This also has to do with the fact that nowadays a water-based paint is used, which does not have the malleability of the old cellulose or synthetic paints that were common in my day. It is even possible that today, many dents are sucked out with special tools that have been developed over the years.

There was a section in the Paint Shop that looked after all the chassis' components which were produced in the Press Shop. These components were always painted in a chassis black finish that had an anti-corrosion additive added to the compound.

The chassis were painted using a dip that was produced in-house. They were hung on special hooks on a conveyer belt-type of set-up that took each chassis through a five-feet-deep trough and immersed it completely in the dip. This allowed all the paint to flow into every single nook and cranny during the immersion, and then any excess would drip off as soon as the conveyer belt lifted them out. From here, the chassis would be transported to an oven which it would pass through and then an enamel paint would be baked onto it at the correct temperature required.

I remember one incident when I was copying the other guys and driving a car with the bonnet up leaning out of the driver's door to gain as much vision as possible when someone parked a car to my right (as it was a left-hand drive car) and as the driver got out, I caught the open door with the front bumper and did quite a lot of damage to the other car. I remember my colleagues telling me that I would have to report it to the Superintendent and to explain to him what I had done. The superintendent was Mr Miserable himself and he gave me such a bollocking that I remember it to this day. Needless to say, I did not make the same mistake again, which I expected was what he was trying to install on me.

Service Department

All apprentices carried out a six-month stint in the Service Department as the technical content was extremely high and complex. However, we all loved it as in essence the work accomplished in this department, such as stripping engines and rebuilding them, was what we all felt that the apprenticeship should be about.

The Service Department was actually involved in looking after the customers' cars, which meant that anyone who preferred the manufacturer rather than the dealer to service or repair their car could come to us. The only downside to this for the client was that it was a lot more expensive to bring the car to the workshop in Abingdon rather than to one of the dealers on the network.

A number of customers chose to come to us as they owned older models or had twin cam engines, which required a lot more expertise on the part of the mechanic to fix. After a while, the staff working at the dealers lacked the knowledge to repair older or more technical models of car, in which case clients were obliged to come to us anyway.

As mentioned previously, a lot of our time in this department was spent stripping and rebuilding engines. Back then, it was always more practical, efficient and cheap to rebuild an engine rather than replace it, which is common practice today.

There was one occasion that I'll never forget, despite the fact that it happened all those years ago. Some things, especially when they involve a huge bollocking, are never erased from your mind!

We had just rebuilt the engine on a MGA Twin Cam and were returning it to its wheels. I was in the process of putting the off-side front wheel back on. The wheel had what we called in the trade 'knock-on wheel nuts', which you had to knock back on with a big copper mallet as it didn't cause any damage to the chrome on the wheel nut. George, the guy that I was working with, warned me to be careful because if you miss the nut and hit the car, you could end up wrecking it.

Well, George should have just kept his mouth shut because no sooner as he uttered these fatal words, I missed the nut and smashed the mallet into the wing of the car. To say that George was angry is an understatement. He went absolutely bananas, hollering that he'd just that second told me to be careful. I was immediately ordered to report to the foreman and tell him what I'd done.

The foreman wasn't too impressed either, and after hearing my account informed me that if I ever made the same mistake again, that meant that I was a lousy mechanic and I would find it nigh on impossible to find employment as one.

Needless to say, I never made the same mistake again, and, obviously, the damage was righted before returning it to the client.

Competitions Department

The Competitions Department was considered by all the apprentices to be one of the best departments in the whole factory, and it was a real bonus that we went straight from the Service Department to this one. We spent an action-packed six months in the Competitions Department due to the high level of technical skills involved, and all dreamt of ending up here full-time at the end.

It was common knowledge, even to us, that the supervisors always kept a keen eye on all the apprentices for the duration of their time in the department as they were constantly on the lookout for new mechanics. Employees came and went and the department was continually expanding the more successful it became. Being offered a job in the Competitions Department was actually a possibility for many of us, which is why we ensured that we were on the ball at all times.

The department worked as a team and its main task consisted of preparing rally cars for BMC (and later British Leyland). The models that we generally dealt with included the Mini Cooper S, the Austin Healey 3000 and the MGB.

I was placed with a terrific guy called Brian Moylan. He was the longest-serving mechanic at the factory and probably one of the most experienced in the department. Brian and I hit it off immediately and it wasn't long before he allowed me to help out in a number of the tasks he was involved with on building a car for the Monte Carlo Rally.

Obviously, I must have made an impression as three months later, when the cars returned from Monte Carlo, I was asked to rebuild one of the Minis that was going to be used as a recce car for the Tulip Rally.

First of all, I removed the engine and gearbox, stripped them both and then rebuilt them as necessary, replacing all the vital parts. The next step was to remove the front sub-frame, which I checked to ensure that no stress cracks had developed in certain areas. I examined all the suspension parts and replaced those that showed signs of damage or the usual wear and tear, and then I did the same with all the ancillary parts that were in doubt. The same procedure was carried out to the rear sub-frame, which I also stripped and rebuilt as necessary. I then changed the hydrolastic units as these always took a real hammering. These units were made out of different material than the standard production units as they had a special diaphragm fitted.

I carried all this out with Brian working in the next bay. If I stumbled across any problem, he would always help me out and guide me back onto the correct path with what I was doing. I completed the task within the allotted time and the car completed the recce without incident.

Brian taught me an awful lot during my time in the Competitions Department, both technically and how the department functioned in itself. Perhaps if it wasn't for him, I might not have been employed and become part of the Competitions Department team two years later.

Drawing Office

Whilst MG was part of the BMC group, and later to become British Leyland, it was totally self-sufficient. All technical drawings were produced at Abingdon by the Drawing Office department with the exception of items such as engines, transmissions and final drives, which were built in factories located in Coventry or Birmingham. The technical drawings for them were produced in their respective factories.

We only spent three months working in the Drawing Office department and during this period we worked alongside one of the section managers. I was placed with the body section and my biggest achievement there was that I drew and designed the rear tail light plinth for the MGA Mark III which went into production on one of the many facelifts the model was subjected to.

It was around this time that I realized that I had to do something about getting a driving license. The sister of my girlfriend then had just passed her test after being taught by a family friend, Harold, who just happened to work on the elevated section of the MGB line, fitting one side of the rear axle. I approached him and asked him if he would teach me as well. Harold agreed, I think due to the fact that he was single and didn't have much to keep him occupied after work in the evenings. Anyway, over the next couple of weeks he took me out in his Morris Minor 1000 two or three times a week, ensuring that we'd stop off each time at a village pub for a quick drink – him, not me!

The lessons went really well and it wasn't long before I applied for my test. I'd heard that there was a massive backlog at the office that dealt with issuing the dates for people's driving tests, and I was expecting to wait at least a couple more months before I got mine after what everyone had been telling me. Fortunately, I didn't have to wait very long at all. I was given a test date just a few weeks' away, which I was totally chuffed about, not to mention extremely surprised about too. Harold and I agreed that I should step the lessons up over the next couple of weeks to ensure that I was 100% ready.

The grand day arrived and, needless to say, I was a nervous wreck. The intensity of my nerves increased the closer it got to the time I was due to sit in the 'hot seat'. As we set off for the test centre in Banbury Road, Oxford, I was sweating profusely.

The actual test went incredibly well. That is apart from the few seconds in which I had to navigate around a cyclist that had pulled out of a busy junction towards the end of my test. Up until this point I was feeling pretty confident that I would pass, but afterwards I thought my chances had been reduced drastically, and that I'd most likely fail. Harry had also witnessed the cyclist incident and was also convinced that I'd fail! However, to my delight, and both our surprise, the examiner contacted me and told me I had passed my driving test.

I now had obtaining my driving license all sewn up, so it was time to start dreaming about my first ever car.

Development Department

This was another department in which apprentices spent a six-month period due to its intricate technical content. During this period we worked with several people within the section who taught us different aspects about the work. The department itself was responsible for solving any of the production problems that had been encountered and also for the development of future enhancements. These enhancements were always unveiled in August, which was the start of the new model year, and still is, as far as I know.

In the Development Department we got involved in looking after engines and transmissions, body modifications and all the ancillary material, and in fitting and testing new equipment.

During my time here, the department was in the middle of developing the new emission system for North America after a law that aimed to reduce carbon-dioxide emissions from all new imported vehicles had just been introduced.

By installing a separate air pump that had the sole purpose of pumping a greater amount of air into the inlet manifold, a reduction of carbon-dioxide emissions was achieved.

This all took place in 1963 and, at that time, North America was the only country concerned with emissions. Thankfully today a lot more countries are preoccupied with carbon-dioxide emissions and their effect on the environment and our health.

One day, I was asked to accompany Tommy Haig, the chief tester for the department, on a day's testing of new models. Tommy, like Eddie Burnell, who I mentioned previously, was highly admired for his driving ability.

Tommy often went to the high-speed testing circuit at MIRA in Northampton, which was run by the motor industry and used by all the motor manufacturers to test the durability, emissions and braking of their new vehicles.

This work was 'top secret' and had to be guarded away from prying eyes. Needless to say, cameras were not allowed into the grounds, and if you were carrying one, it had to be passed over to security on entrance and was returned when you left.

High-speed testing was possible due to the fact that the circuit had been constructed with a high-speed banking around its perimeter. This meant that the faster you went, the higher up the banking the vehicle travelled, which could be quite frightening to a passer-by, despite the fact that it would be impossible to actually carry out this kind of testing on any public road.

On this particular day, our task was to take an MG Midget, which the Development Department had prepared on a prototype body shell for the Sebring 12-hour event in America, whose 1275 engine was misfiring at high speed. It was thought that the misfiring was a result of the spark plug becoming ineffective when it reached a specific heat range.

On route, we called in at the home of the racing representative of Champion Spark Plugs, whose name unfortunately escapes me. He had in his possession every single spark plug to suit all the various heat ranges that we required. We selected a number of spark plugs which we assumed would cover all aspects and, therefore, solve the problem.

This done, I thought we'd be off, but what I didn't know was that this guy and Tommy were actual drinking buddies and great pals. So, after a few Scotches, which at the age of 20 I wasn't used to drinking, Tommy finally decided that it was in fact time to leave as we still had to get to MIRA. The drink-driving laws were obviously much more relaxed in those days, as the thought of drinking and driving didn't seem to worry us at all.

When we arrived at MIRA we checked in with administration and were promptly sent to the high-speed circuit. It wasn't long before we were lapping at 130 mph, which wasn't the best activity after a couple of drinks.

Luckily, the trip was not a wasted one and we did solve the problem of the misfiring engine. It took several spark plug changes and God knows how many laps around the circuit before we found the correct plug to withstand the heat range for the speeds that we were driving.

On the way home we stopped off at the Green Man pub just outside Silverstone and I wasn't surprised to learn that Tommy knew the landlord very well. So, after several pints in this place, Tommy decided it was about time we returned to Abingdon, which we did at around 7 p.m. enabling me to claim two hours overtime – you could call it compensation for my inebriated state and sore head.

In any case, my journey was still not over that night as I had to ride home on my bike, which turned out to be a real struggle as I had to put all my energy and focus into staying upright. When I got home, Mum had dinner ready on the table, which I ate and promptly fell asleep in the chair straight after. This, in turn, had my mum worried sick as she thought I was ill and coming down with something. However, I believe it was my elder brother John who set her straight and put her mind at rest as he himself had worked in the same department as Tommy for a number of years and experienced similar days out with him!

And, while I would in no way advocate drinking on the job, the Midget that we worked on actually performed really well in the Sebring 12-hour event race, and won its class.

Planning Office

The Planning Office was responsible for the upkeep of the factory and dealt with any modernization that was required to any of the buildings. There was no motor vehicle technology training involved here at all, but we spent three months in this department anyway. This was so that we could see how important this department was to the factory, especially to the Production Department and the production lines.

The Planning Office had its own drawing office in which all the technical drawings for any building work or alterations to any building were carried out.

There were only seven people working in the Planning Office: two draughtsmen, two carpenters, two painters and a bricklayer. My three months here were quite enjoyable, although not as much laughter went on here as it did in other departments. Everyone in the Planning Office was very serious, unlike everyone else.

Conducted Tours of the MG Factory

The Personnel Department always had one employee who acted as the apprentice administrator, but also doubled up as the factory guide. His job as a guide was to organize conducted tours around the factory to any visiting groups. If the touring party consisted of more than ten people, then, for safety purposes, the group was divided into two and a second person was required to help show the party around.

This second tour guide was always selected from the senior apprentices, of which there were three or four of us in the same year that shared the role. I used to enjoy this part of the job because we were required to go home and change into respectable clothes. At some point during the tour, we'd also end up in the management restaurant for lunch or tea and cakes, which was a great added bonus. If we were really lucky, we'd finish the tour half an hour before the factory closed for the day, which meant we could clock out 30 minutes early as there was no point in changing back into our overalls to do less than an hour's work — that was our excuse anyway!

The Last Three Months

At some point during the last three months of our apprenticeship we would discuss the options available to us at the factory with the Personnel Department. We would tell them in which department we'd most like to work, and they would inform us of what was available. The two didn't necessarily always match. However, vacancies were always arising, so you generally wouldn't have to wait too long until another post needed filling.

When I finished my apprenticeship, the only vacancy available was in the Show Department. It could have been worse and working in the Show Department had one huge advantage: there was plenty of opportunity for doing lots of overtime, which, because of our exceptionally low wages as an apprenticeship, was a godsend.

In October 1963, I was part of the team that manned our stand at the Motor Show in Earl's Court and was employed to participate for the duration of the show. We worked

Monday to Saturday and as soon as the show closed at 7 p.m. at the end of the week, we'd all go straight home as we were too exhausted to do anything else.

When the show finished for the week on Saturday 24 October, however, we drove home and decided to stop off for a drink just outside Henley-on-Thames. I eventually arrived home about midnight only for my father to unexpectedly pass away just ten minutes later from a coronary thrombosis. Needless to say, I didn't return to the Motor Show the following week, which was fraught with making the necessary arrangements for his funeral with my brothers as well as trying to come to terms with the fact that I'd never see my dad again. I was just six months away from my 21st birthday. Losing a parent at such a young age, when they are relatively young themselves, is hard to bear, and, I have to admit, that I missed my father terribly then, and still do.

Educational Visits

Very often, the Personnel Department would organize an educational visit for the apprentices to go on. We'd head off for the day to see how other factories belonging to the group worked. We would often visit some of our suppliers, such as Joseph Lucas, Dunlop Tyres or one of the paint manufacturers. These were always interesting and fun days out, despite the fact that we had to be accompanied by someone from another department who would act as supervisor – and taxi driver as he had to drive us there and back.

Once, and I'm not really sure why, we were taken to visit the RAF Brize Norton, an American air base just outside of Witney in Oxford. We were shown around the radar and air traffic control departments, but weren't allowed anywhere near the aircraft, which disappointed me hugely. Nevertheless, it was an interesting tour nonetheless.

On occasions, we would be seconded to one of the other BMC factories for two or three weeks, which was extremely instructive as we would return having gained knowledge and experience in new things.

Once, I spent three weeks at the Longbridge production plant in Birmingham and worked in the trim shop, foundry, body pressings and body assembly departments – all areas that we didn't have at Abingdon. Unlike our factory, the production lines in Longbridge were fully automated, which made me wonder exactly how long the factory at Abingdon would stay open for.

I also spent two weeks at the engines division in Coventry and got to see how a cylinder block was machined, bored, drilled and measured, and then how all the single components came together for the final engine assembly.

Another fascinating sight was seeing a con-rod in a drop-forge condition undergoing all its various machine operations and eventually being assembled onto the pistons and fitted into the engine. And, the crankshaft was a similar procedure as that too was drop forged and required quite a lot of intricate machining before it was ready to be placed in the cylinder block.

The worst secondment by far was at the foundry in Nuneaton. It was noisy and extremely dirty – kind of what you would expect working in the motor industry, but multiplied by a thousand.

However, this is where we saw how a cylinder head and cylinder block mold were made from sand and molten metal, which was poured into a cylinder block casting mold. The metal was left to cool and then the sand was removed from the casting by a huge vibrating machine. The casting was then taken to the fettling shop where an operator ground off all the excess metal and subsequently, it was put through a cleaning process of high-pressure air and water, which removed any remaining excess sand from the waterways or oil galleries. The final step was to take the molded item to the machine shop where it would be prepared for the relevant factory to finalize it and assemble it.

There were actually four of us that went to work at the foundry in Nuneaton. Me, Derek Plummer, Derek Powell and Mick Hogan. We were all put into the same accommodation that the company had allocated for us, which was owned by a real dragon of a lady who laid down the law the minute we set foot onto her premises.

Anyhow, we'd only been in our room for an hour when we managed to break the bed. One of the boys pushed another, who lost his balance and fell onto the bed, causing it to break. The landlady raced upstairs to our room to find out what all the noise was about and appeared at our door in a matter of moments.

My quick thinking probably saved us from being kicked out there and then. I swiftly removed my trousers, opened our bedroom door and greeted her in my underpants. Confronted by this sight, she decided to retreat and talk to us from the landing, thus the sight of her broken piece of furniture eluded her.

We decided to hide the broken leg by putting one of our suitcases under it to hold it up and managed to get away with that. We worked out what we would need to fix the leg and brought all the tools and necessary equipment back with us from home when we returned after the weekend. We fixed the leg and returned all the tools first thing Monday morning to the car without anyone, including the landlady, being none the wiser.

Rag Week

Every year, all the major companies in the Abingdon area that had taken on apprentices used to organize a rag week for charity, and every night there would be something different on.

One of our favourite events was the pram race. The race started at the bottom of Ock Street in Abingdon and the route would follow the road into town and go all the way around the one-way system. The rules were very straightforward: the pram must be occupied at all times by a member of the team.

So, the race consisted of pushing the pram from pub to pub until you reached the finishing line. However, at each pub, whoever was inside the pram had to get out, down half a pint of bitter, jump back in the pram and continue the ride until the next pub where the next member of the team would down the drink, and so on.

Now, Abingdon had 44 public houses on this route in those days and there were six people in each team. It doesn't take a genius to work out that by the time we reached the finishing line, each and every member of the team was actually pretty pissed. This meant lots of merriness, giggling, unstableness and frequent outbursts of laughter.

Despite the fact that the pram had been modified and strengthened for the purposes of the race, it was invariably unusable afterwards due to ending up with buckled wheels, a twisted chassis and totally distorted.

On the Saturday evening of rag week, we always held a large procession of floats that paraded through the centre of Abingdon for a number of hours. To make up the numbers, girls from the office would be invited to join us on the float and to walk alongside collecting money. This event was also a competition to see who could design and produce the best float as voted for by a panel of judges.

One year, we decked out our float, which was the back of an MG lorry, as a massive and very elaborate pirates' ship and the driver gave up his Saturday evening to chauffeur us around town for the duration of the parade. In a bid to outdo the other entrants and win the judges' votes, we asked the girls to wear the shortest miniskirts without going too over the top. It worked. Well, I don't know if it was the girls' miniskirts, but our float was voted the most imaginative of all and we won the competition. Needless to say, there was plenty of celebrating and drinking that night as well.

Abingdon Polytechnic & Oxford College of Art & Commerce

As part of our apprenticeship, we had to attend a day-release course at one of the local colleges. My first year was spent at the Abingdon Polytechnic. The course was great, however, I didn't get on with one teacher there in particular. God knows what my older brother Bill had got up to before me, but the teacher certainly hadn't forgotten our family name. Nevertheless, somehow or another, I did actually pass the end-of-year exam, which then enabled me to progress and take the City & Guilds course.

It's always as you get older that you begin to reflect on the earlier events of your life and picture how you could have done things better. Well, it was at this early stage of my life that I wished I had paid more attention to studying at school. I'm sure I would have found college so much easier and less of a struggle, and it may well have prevented me from having to repeat the final year.

One of the positive aspects of going to college as opposed to spending all week inside the factory was that there were women milling about at college. It didn't take me and my friend long to get to know a few of them. A number of girls were nurses and my friend and I were invited to some of the dances held at the nurses' home in Slade on several occasions. The dances were always held on a Friday evening and attendance was by invite only. The fact that there was habitually a shortage of fellers at these events meant that me and my mate were generally in for a good night. This can more or less be translated into us staying the night with one of the nurses at their quarters and having to sneak out early in the morning before the warden came on duty. I attended dozens of these dances and made sure that I always picked a friend with a car to come with me, especially as it wasn't much fun being stranded in Slade at seven in the morning without any transport.

I remember one night I returned to the nurses' quarters and the girl I was with instructed me to be very quiet when we entered her room. I soon realized why when I spotted her roommate fast asleep in the next bed. However, as we began to make love, I noted not one pair of hands on me, but two. Glancing over my shoulder, I saw that her roommate had obviously woken up, moved over into our bed and begun to join in the fun – just as I was reaching climax with the first girl. Although I had finished with the first girl and was extremely content, it was clear that the second girl wasn't going anywhere, or going to allow me to go anywhere either. I got my breath back and then started again, this time with the second girl. Thankfully, I didn't leave either of them disappointed that night.

Sports

When I was 18, I joined the Abingdon Rowing Club with a couple of mates and made up a coxed four skull team. We trained two or three times a week, and it wasn't long before we entered several Head of the River Races in Oxford and other venues around the country.

In 1961, we entered a number of regattas too, one of them being the Maidenhead Regatta, which was organized by the Burway Rowing Club. When we arrived on the morning of the race, we saw that there were 20 entries for our event. This meant a tough day ahead because if we did well, we'd have to race at least four times that day. Each race was 1,000 metres, with each one becoming progressively more difficult and competitive than the last.

We won the first race by an easy margin of one and a half boat lengths. This took us up into the second round and, again, we won that race, albeit by a smaller margin of just a few yards. The third race was tough, but our adrenalin had kicked in by then and we were running on overdrive. This was the semi-final and turned out to be a real nail biter. We quickly took the lead, but then were overtaken by the other team, who remained in the winning position right up until the last few seconds. With three minutes to spare our cox increased the stroke speed to 26 and with every ounce of strength and determination within our bodies, we managed to pull back the lead and win the race by just four metres.

This meant that we had reached the final and we were

determined that we would not let the other team beat us. As soon as the whistle blew to start the race, we were off. The race passed by in a blur, but the whole team was entirely focused on reaching the finishing line before the other team and took no notice of anything else around. As we had pictured in our mind's eye, we crossed the line first and didn't even catch a glimpse of the other team until they followed up and finished the race behind us. As you can probably expect by now, we managed to sink a few pints that night in true victorious and celebratory fashion.

At this time of my life I was still playing football for Abingdon United, however, MG's wanted me to play for them. Their first team was in the first division of the Isthmian League, while their second team played in the first division of the North Berkshire Football League. I decided to take the leap the following year and left Abingdon United to go and play for MG's second team.

I also used to enjoy playing table tennis as a hobby and decided to form a team with a few friends. We managed to get into the Oxford league, but, unfortunately, didn't do very well and gave up after a couple of years. We did have a lot of fun, though, and enjoyed travelling to different locations and areas and mixing with different people.

One of my old schoolteachers also persuaded me to play rugby for Abingdon Town. This lasted just one season as I found the game too rough. Not only that, but I couldn't afford the drinking sessions after each match on my apprentice's salary.

Eskdale Outward Bound Course - 1961

During my apprenticeship the company sent me to Seascale in Eskdale, Cumbria to go on one of their one-month Outward Bound leadership courses, which actually forms part of the Duke of Edinburgh Award. The course was excellent as it was designed to quickly build up your self-confidence, but I openly admit it was also very tough.

When we arrived, we were divided into groups of ten and allocated a dormitory. Each dormitory housed five bunk beds. In addition, we were handed a housekeeping cleaning rota. This consisted of a plan of the communal areas within the centre and on it the dates and times of when we were responsible for cleaning. After cleaning each area, it would be inspected by one of the instructors, most of whom were ex-military, which gives you some idea of how thorough we had to be with our cleaning!

As well as the communal areas, we also had to clean our dormitories. During our induction we were all given a lesson on how to make a bed. Then we had to have a go at making one in front of all the others on the course. If anyone made a mistake after being shown how to do it by the instructor, he would rip off all the bed clothes off every single bed, not just the offending one, and we would have to make them all again.

The course was held at a mountaineering centre in the Lake District, and I remember that during our first week there we spent three entire days searching for a couple of climbers that had gone missing the day before we arrived. The weather was not great for climbing, nor searching, for that matter, as it had been raining continuously for several days beforehand. One group did eventually find the climbers at the bottom of a precipice, but they had died. The worst thing was that the doctor told us that they had only been dead for approximately seven hours. It was a horrible thought to think that if we'd found them earlier, we might have saved their lives.

Already by the second week, the course was starting to get more serious and very strenuous. We were woken up every morning at 6 a.m. sharp and started the day with a run. Now, this wasn't your average run around the block a few times, this was slightly more difficult than that. We were made to run around a huge lake. Halfway around the lake there was an impressive waterfall with water that flowed down from the top of the mountain. Anyone that has bathed in mountain water knows that it is absolutely hideously freezing cold. Anyway, our task each morning was to run round the lake until we arrived at the waterfall. Then, we had to stand under the water, fully clothed in our gym kits, and turn around three times. This was done under the watchful eye of the instructor, who made you repeat the process if you faltered in any way. Once completed to his satisfaction, we would then have to run back to the dormitory, change out of our wet clothes and shower and dress very quickly. The process finished by making our beds and tidying our dormitory before inspection, which was difficult in itself after ten dripping bodies had passed through to get to the shower. If we passed the inspection, it was only then that we were allowed to make our way to the dining room for a well-deserved hearty breakfast.

While we did our upmost to ensure that our cleaning was faultless, you could guarantee that on a daily basis someone would fail the inspection. This is because whoever did would have to wash up for 60 people and clean the toilets and showers – tasks that had to be carried out on a daily basis anyway.

Also during the second week, we were given some basic training on how to survive out in the wild and the necessary skills required, which would all come in handy for a forthcoming activity. At the end of the week, we spent three days with our instructor walking across the fells. This was an exercise in map-reading, using a compass and learning to recognize the various landmarks around us. What we didn't realize was that this was all essential to a similar exercise we would have to carry out. The only difference with the second exercise was that we would have to complete it totally solo – no group, no instructor, just ourselves for company! The plus side was that after having been involved in the mountain rescue in the first week of our stay, we all took it very seriously and focused 100% on what we were being taught.

So, off we all set in the third week on a solo expedition that lasted for 24 hours. We were handed the route and two map references. The first was a checkpoint where we would meet up with our instructor, and the second pinpointed the area in which they expected us to set up our camp for the night. Due to the fact that we had to carry what we would need for the night's stay in our rucksack along with our sleeping bag, ground sheet and bivouac sheet, I decided to only take a change of clothes and a bar of soap to lessen the load as much as possible. Although we were out on our own and supposedly fending for ourselves, which we did, we were unaware that the instructors were actually following each one of us to make sure that we did stick to the instructions given and not take any shortcuts. This was a great exercise in learning how to fend for yourself, but, as well as that, it was also probably the first time in my life that I'd spent a full 24 hours on my own.

I found the first map reference easily and waited for my instructor to turn up, which he did after about half an hour. He was so impressed with my efforts that he decided to change the map reference where I was due to set up camp for a new one, which was about another two miles further from the original. I planned this route carefully as the instructor had repositioned my new site over on the other side of the river, which meant that I either had to swim to cross over to the other side or locate some kind of bridge or crossing. Studying the map, I worked out that the nearest bridge was approximately five miles downstream. Well, I wasn't having that so I scanned the map even more thoroughly and noticed a couple of dotted lines that crossed over the river about a mile downstream. As the camp was located in the opposite direction, I suspected that the instructor would not expect me to look at the possibilities of taking the downstream route seeing as it seemed to lead me away from the camp site.

I decided to go for it anyway and reminded myself that if the plan failed, I'd have to walk an extra couple of miles.

When I arrived at the reference point, I was delighted to find a small but very old pedestrian bridge that looked as if it was no longer being used. Despite its shaky appearance, I presumed that if it posed any real danger of collapsing, there would be some sort of notice or sign in place to warn people. I opted to take the chance and make the crossing. As soon as I set foot on the bridge, it began to creak. Nevertheless, I carried on and edged my way down the bridge. Despite the continual swaying and groaning as I made my way along the rickety contraption, I finally made it to the other side and was delighted that I had saved myself the five-mile walk. I arrived at the camp site a good few hours earlier than both my instructor and I had expected.

Later on, I learned that all of my colleagues had been faced with the same problem of having to cross the river. They, however, had decided to wade through the water, meaning that once across they were faced with another problem – one of wet clothes and how to get them dry again.

I set about building my camp with the four pieces of equipment that had been given to me: a bivouac sheet, a ground sheet, a sleeping bag and a small container to boil water in to make a hot drink and cook the provisions we had been provided with. When I had passed by the river earlier on, the forethought of collecting some of the water came to me as it had appeared so exceptionally clean, plus I didn't know if there were any sources of water near to or at the campsite. Our provisions given to us before we set off only consisted of a couple of biscuits, tea, sugar and the 'pièce de résistance' – an egg. The egg was only useful, however, if it didn't break on route, as it wasn't hard-boiled;

it was uncooked. I had packed mine inside my mug together with the tea and sugar and, fortunately, it was still intact when I arrived.

I had noticed that there were a lot of rabbits running around the camping area, so I decided to set a snare in the hope of catching one that I would be able to cook and eat for dinner later that night. The thought of dining on just one egg did not fill me with great anticipation of a good and filling meal.

Anyway, I sat extremely still, barely moving a muscle, for about an hour and a half when a rabbit suddenly caught my eye. It was sniffing around the snare, inching its way forward with every second until it was too late – for the rabbit, that is. I killed it quickly to stop it from suffering. I didn't really think about my actions while I was doing this as I'd never killed a rabbit before. The next step was to skin and clean it, which was a slightly easier task as I was able to recall how my father used to do it. Before I could cook the animal, I had to find a nice stick to use as a spit and build a fire that would last long enough to cook it. I completed both of these tasks and cooked the rabbit to perfection over the hot coals of the barbeque. I discovered that rabbit is a fantastic meat to cook on a barbeque due to the fact that it contains very little fat. This means that the meat can be cooked very evenly as the temperature of the fire is maintained at the same heat because there is no dripping fat to raise it.

That evening, the instructor showed up just as I was about to tuck into my rabbit dinner, which was in fact extremely tasty and much-needed after the day's adventure. He was actually flabbergasted at the sight of me and the set-up I had going on there, although I think he tried to hide it at the time. It wasn't until much later that he admitted to me that he thought I would fail the test altogether because of my carefree attitude. It appeared that I was more ready for it than he had ever imagined as I also found out later that out of the 40 students, the other 39 had not been as lucky with their food situation and had only eaten the rations that they had been given.

During our final week of the course, we had to accomplish a similar exercise. However, in this case, we went out in groups of five and camped out for three nights, not just one. Unfortunately, I was appointed the team leader. I say unfortunately because I was up for some fun and a bit of a lark with the other guys, but being made team leader prevented me from doing so as I had to act responsibly. My team's safety was in my hands.

There were several checkpoints on this occasion and we were given a number of map references too, but this time the route covered a distance of about 60 miles across some of the highest peaks in the Lake District, which made map-reading slightly tougher.

During the second day, one of my team members slipped and cut his hand badly. We weren't in a position to get him to a hospital or to make a phone call, so we just had dress the wound at regular intervals, ensure that he kept it clean and generally look after him, making certain he didn't slip again.

As soon as we arrived at the camping spot for that night, I made sure that I set up the injured lad's tent first. We then got a fire going to keep him warm, in particular, and so we could all get a hot drink down us after the trek. Even before I set up my own bivouac, I made the injured lad change out of his wet clothes and into some dry ones. I suspected that he was beginning to suffer from shock, so I asked one of the other lads to sit with him and keep him talking while we filled him up with lots of hot, sweet tea.

The next morning, the lad seemed much more positive and was very grateful to all of us for how we had looked after him. We still had another two days to go, though, so we still kept a close eye on him just in case.

My group sailed through the four days and three nights and passed the test with flying colours. We caught a couple of rabbits and a small muntjac deer and didn't go hungry once. Some of the team were opposed to eating the game we'd caught, but as soon as their eyes feasted on us tucking into our food, they soon changed their minds.

What we really should have suspected, but didn't, was that we weren't completely on our own. The whole time, our instructors were spying on our every move, just like Big Brother, through binoculars and keeping a close eye on our antics. This didn't matter though as we scored highly in the way that we looked after our injured friend and set about getting food for the camp. If anything, being scrutinized to that extent probably acted in our favour.

Motor Shows

As an apprentice, we were always allowed to visit the International Motor Show held at the Exhibition Centre in Earl's Court, London. The company would pack us off with the train fare and some money from expenses that we could buy a snack with. On one occasion I remember taking my girlfriend at the time, a short girl with big breasts called Joy. Joy was very proud of her large assets and always encouraged me to play with them, which, as you can guess, I never objected to.

We arrived in London and headed to the show first thing. Once there we made sure that we were seen and spoke to everyone that we should have spoken to. After the necessary formalities, however, we were off like a shot to explore what London had to offer. We made our way to Leicester Square and met up with another one of the apprentices and his girlfriend, then we all went to the cinema.

I forget what we saw, or didn't see in this case, but I do remember that the cinema was fairly empty. We sat in the back row and got up to what everyone used to get up to in the back row of the cinema in those days, making sure that we weren't caught at the same time. Within ten minutes of being seated, Joy was already asking me to fondle her breasts, which, of course, I did as I didn't want to disappoint her. If we hadn't been in the cinema, she probably would have persuaded me to go all the way. We did have a laugh that afternoon, though. Joy was one of the noisiest lovers

I've ever had and every time she became aroused while we watched the film, the other people in the audience kept shushing us to be quiet. The constant shushing had us in fits of giggles, which I suppose covered up her constant groaning.

British Leyland Apprentices Continental Tour

Every year, each factory within the BL organization elected one apprentice to go on a continental tour of Holland and Germany where they would visit other motor manufacturers and dealers. The trip was always arranged and coordinated by one of the dealers in both of the other countries, and while the visiting UK group was there, they would always ensure that some of their lads were available to take the visitors out and show them the local sights on the odd occasion that there was a spare evening.

I was in my third year and just 18 years old when the personnel manager sent for me and informed me that I had been selected that year to represent the company at this event. I was so excited I could have almost burst as I had never left the country before to travel abroad. This meant that I would also require my very own passport.

Before we left, we had several briefing sessions at the Longbridge factory in Birmingham during which all the ground rules for our trip were explained to us in minute detail. Obviously, the company's reputation was at stake and the bosses were worried for our safety – as well as the amount of alcohol we were likely to ingest. While these briefings were a tad tedious, they gave us the opportunity to get to know the others going on the trip and from there decide who we were going to share a room with once we had arrived.

There are two things that stand out in my memory from this tour, apart from the great set of lads that I happened to be teamed up with. First of all, during the first leg of our visit to Germany, one of the highlights was undoubtedly speeding down the autobahn in a Ferrari. OK, we weren't actually driving, but the owner of the BL distributorship in Düsseldorf took each and every one of us 18 apprentices, one at a time, for a spin in his Ferrari. He also gave us a guided tour of his dealership, which was extremely informative as most of us had never been behind the scenes of one before and it was interesting to learn the ins and outs of the business. And, to finish off the morning, he took us for a fabulous slap-up meal after which we returned to the hotel at around 5 p.m.

But the day wasn't over just yet. Later that evening, we went out for a meal with a couple of the apprentices from the distributor, who then took us to the local legalised brothel. Needless to say, we were all gobsmacked by the sights before us and the propositions made to us. I think it can be fair to say that none of us had seen anything like that before.

Fortunately, an apprentice's wage did not provide us with spare money to spend on that type of activity. And, we weren't about to put that type of entertaining onto our expenses sheet for the company to pay for. We went home having looked but not touched, and I must point out that visiting the brothel was only an educational visit, not a practical one.

The second part of the trip in Holland followed a similar pattern minus the ride in the Ferrari. We did, however, go out one night with the local apprentices who were keen to introduce us to their alcoholic speciality, strawberry wine. I stuck to the beer as the wine was way too sweet for me, but most of the other lads liked it – and got completely wasted on it too.

All in all, the trip was a huge success and I really appreciated the opportunity to travel abroad and get to mix and make friends with young people of the same age, but who came from a different country.

A Lesson to Be Learned

Another instructive incident I remember was when I was around 19 years old. I was on my way to my girlfriend's house in Radley, near Kennington in Oxford, and it was snowing hard. I was travelling on my bike and I had to keep my head down most of the journey to keep the snow from falling into my eyes.

All of a sudden I came to a dramatic standstill as I had cycled into the back of a parked car. The jolt catapulted me from the seat of my bike onto the roof of the car. Unfortunately, that was not the end of the matter because the collision had damaged the boot, roof panel and bumper of the parked vehicle. In those days there was no hit and run, and I remember sheepishly knocking on the door of the house in front of which the car was parked in a bid to find the owner and explain to him what had happened. The owner of the car took my details and said that he would be in touch.

A few weeks later he turned up at my house with an estimate for how much it would cost to repair the damage. Fortunately for me, my Aunt Vera answered and suggested that it might be better if he put the claim through his insurance company as I didn't have that sort of money. She did propose that I pay him a couple of pounds a month for the next few of years, which he did not really appreciate and, luckily, he did decide in the end to go with his insurance company. Needless to say, I was always extremely careful when cycling in the snow from then on.

The Apprentices' Association

The company had its very own Apprentices' Association who always organized a number of social events throughout the year. These were generally well-attended and the profits made at the smaller events, like the discos held in the MG Social Club, helped pay for the annual dinner and dance, which was always held in the Royce Rooms in Abingdon. The managing director, personnel director, apprentice master and the apprentice coordinator were always invited to this event together with their wives. However, the fact that the members of management were present didn't stop us from consuming way too much alcohol, and it was a given that someone somewhere would get into some form of trouble. During the last year of my apprenticeship, I was voted in as chairman of this association.

Show Department

As I previously mentioned, the only available vacancy at the time when I was nearing the end of my apprenticeship was in the Show Department. This department prepared vehicles or displays for the relevant motor shows and dealer showrooms. This department was also in charge of looking after all the company demonstrators plus a collection of vintage cars that the company owned.

The first job I was involved in was to prepare an MGB for the forthcoming motor show to be held at Earl's Court. I was instructed to cut the car in half from the front to the back using the centre of the car as a datum point. Then, I had to make good all the areas that had been sectioned so that during the exhibition the car could be opened up with the aid of two strategically placed hydraulic rams to display both halves of the vehicle with all the components sectioned along with the body shell.

The sectioning of the car turned out to be quite a job because it meant that the engine, gearbox and final drive all had to be cut in half, as they fell on the centre line, along with the components that fell in this area too. In order to prevent certain parts from coming away or from falling apart, we had to peg or glue them. In addition, any part that had been sectioned had to be finished off well, which was done by painting a red line on the component to denote the cut.

Some parts were more difficult than others, but I think the engine gave me the biggest problem. I made the cut on the datum line, but this was not in the centre of the engine due to the engine being slightly off set. This resulted in one half of the pistons being held firmly in the cylinder bore, but the other portion of the piston, which ended up as less than half of it, had to be pegged to the cylinder wall in order to keep it in position. Many components had to be pegged in this way, meaning that the whole job was extremely time-consuming. Some days it was impossible to even see how much progress had been made, it was that slow!

The gearbox was also slightly problematic as the casing was cut on the datum line, yet the gears were left intact. To get them working for when the car was opened up, an electric motor was installed. This also affected the final drive, which had to be operational in conjunction with the gearbox.

Nevertheless, by the end of the task, the display did look fantastic, if I say so myself, and it was all fully operational. The completed piece was, in fact, the centrepiece of the MG Car Company exhibition stand at the 1964 Motor Show held in Earl's Court.

The manager of the Show Department was a man that I struggled to understand, and get on with. I think the same could be said for him about me. I entered into numerous arguments and confrontations with him because he always seemed to look after his favourites and disregard the others, which, as you might have guessed, included me. I don't think he lost any sleep when I moved on to another department.

My fiancée and I decided to get married a month before my 21st birthday, and my mother agreed that we should go and live with her in Selwood Road until our house in Grove, near Wantage in Berkshire, was finished. As well as saving a bit of money living with Mum, it was also a chance for her to have some much-needed company as she was still trying to come to terms with the loss of my father.

Our new house was finally completed in September 1964 and we moved into Minns Road in Wantage straightaway. This turned out to be an extra blessing as Tom, a mechanic from the Competitions Department, lived just three doors away. Tom later became a very good friend and work colleague of mine with whom I spent a lot of time travelling all over the world on business, not to say that we didn't have plenty of fun at the same time.

Competitions Department

After three months working in the Show Department, I was summoned to Personnel and told that there was a vacancy in the Competitions Department for a skilled mechanic and that the department had requested that the job be offered to me.

It was every mechanic's dream to be employed in the Competitions Department, working on rally and race cars every single day. At this point, I was 21 years old, and I can tell you that at that age I didn't need much persuading.

I went home that night almost bursting with excitement and pleasure. I had to sit down with my wife, however, and explain to her that my new position, if I agreed to take it, would mean me spending a lot of time away from home. On the plus side, I would be compensated financially for the inconvenience.

We had just taken out a mortgage and spent a lot of money on furniture, so we both saw that the extra wages to be earned could come in very handy. We both decided together that I should go for it and take the new job. Within a week I was working in my new role.

I started on the following Monday, much to the envy of all the other apprentices. My starting salary was £1,200 per annum, but this was dramatically enhanced by the number of overtime hours we were expected to put in when required, together with the pay structure that came into force when we were away at an event. For every day that we were away, we were paid for 13 hours' work instead of eight. This was fine for Monday to Saturday as the total always amounted to the correct 13 hours. However, the going rate for a Sunday was supposed to be double time, but this would have equated to two lots of 13 hours which is 26 hours. Try as we might, even we couldn't convince the powers-that-be that a Sunday consisted of 26 hours whereas all the other days consisted of 24.

In addition to this we were given an out-of-pocket expense of £1.50 for every day that we were away, which was non-accountable. We were also given a daily allowance of £7.50 to cover all meal expenses, together with a lump sum for the events which was to cover what we called 'extraordinary expenses' whilst away. This was accountable, though, and we had to produce receipts for the final analysis. However, it did not take long to work out how to get around the administration of the expense account.

My first job in the department was to build a recce car (a car used for practice) for one of the drivers in the 1965 Monte Carlo Rally. I cannot remember which driver it was to be allocated to, but I do remember being given a very tatty Mini that had just returned from another event.

I set about pulling it apart, rebuilding the engine and gearbox, and overhauling the suspension assemblies as stipulated on the specification and build sheet I had been handed.

This all took about six weeks and on completion I was expected to run the car in to make sure there were no teething problems. I had to clock up 1,500 miles within seven days so that within this time any problems would show up and could be fixed, leaving enough time for the final preparation before taking the car to the event. This was great as I used to travel to and from work in the rally car and drive it about at weekends. This was always the case when working on all the cars in this department.

On some occasions, the car was finished with only a few days to spare before the event. In these cases, we would sort out a rota with some of our other colleagues in the department and we would all take it in turns and have the car on the road for 24 hours a day in order to get the miles on as quickly as possible.

Whenever I built a car and arranged the 24-hour driving rota, I was careful to make sure I never got any of the night shifts as we still had to come into work at the same time as usual the following morning. This plan, however, worked against me when I helped my other colleagues with their 24-hour driving, as they always managed to get me back for the late-night shifts that I'd assigned to them.

Nevertheless, despite the odd day here and there when I wasn't at my most energetic, the benefits from the overtime more than compensated this. The overtime element in this department was twice as great as my contracted salary.

Monte Carlo Rally 1965

I remember my first trip out with the department, which was on the Monte Carlo Rally. It was only the third time that I had been abroad, so I was still a bit green to this travelling business.

The Monte was always a big event for the whole team as all of the staff was involved in one way or another. This year was to be no exception as six Minis were entered, two of which were Group III. This meant a lot of extra hours had to be put in working on these two cars. A great part of the job was to lighten the bodies as much as possible, which meant fitting aluminium doors, bonnet and boot and Perspex doors and rear windows.

I wasn't actually involved in preparing any of the event cars, but when the time came I was instructed to go to Paris with Bill Price and Bob Whittington. They dropped me off in the centre of Paris at the Gare du Nord railway station so that I could catch the night sleeper down to San Rafael where I would be met by one of my other colleagues.

However, we arrived in Paris mid-morning and the train was not due to leave until 9.30 p.m. that evening. That meant I had quite a bit of time to kill, which, I must add, is not such a bad thing to happen in Paris. I had no knowledge of any French at all, other than how to ask for a beer or for my bill in a restaurant, and to this day I firmly believe that the whole scenario was an initiation test to prove to the management that I was capable of surviving on my own in a foreign country.

Believe it or not all went well. I walked for a while and found a good restaurant where I thoroughly enjoyed a lovely meal and then I went to the cinema (and I did not know that they showed that type of film in the early evenings). I eventually got a taxi back to the Gare du Nord where the porter showed me to my cabin and, lo and behold, the train left spot on time.

I was woken up to a loud banging at the door and shouting at about 3.30 a.m. Obviously I had no idea what was going on, so I pulled up the blind and peered out of the window only to find that the train had stopped and was not going any further as it was in a siding. I flung some clothes on in a hurry and sought out the porter, who, on realizing that I did not speak the language, showed me where to go. Apparently I had to change trains, which meant changing platforms as well. Well, I couldn't fault the French rail service as the porter carried my suitcase and led me to the correct platform where the train to San Rafael was waiting to leave.

I finally arrived at San Rafael on time at 8.30 in the morning and my colleague was there to meet me.

Unfortunately, I do not remember much about my activities on this rally due to my memory not being as sharp as I'd like more than for any other reason. However, I do remember that Timo Machinen was the outright winner, the Morley brother finished 27th and Paddy Hopkirk won his class.

The result was well received at Lonbridge and George Harriman, who was the group managing director at the time, sent instructions for a party to be held for all the team and trade support personnel.

The party took place at the Pirate Restaurant in Monte Carlo, and it was a fantastic affair. The majority of us remember two highlights of the evening: Doug Watts riding a donkey around the tables and the sight of Alex Issigonis and Geoff Mabbs balancing on floodlit rocks by the water, swaying to the music while clasping their gin and tonics in their hands and looking as though they would fall into the water at any time.

This was to be my first experience of partying after an event in this style, and, believe me, the guys knew how to party. This event, however, was just one of many during my time in this department.

The win created a tremendous amount of publicity at home, with the winning car and several of the drivers and staff being flown back to the UK to appear on *Sunday Night at the London Palladium*. Our Publicity Department had taken out full-page advertisements in Monday's daily newspapers and weekly journals, and many of the country's best-known journalists were queuing up to road test the cars.

It was on this rally that I first met a Phil, a private entrant, and his wife Pauline. They were from Garforth, near Leeds, and I am delighted to say that Phil and I are still in touch with one another today and we meet up fairly regularly either in the UK or in Spain. Sadly, Pauline, who was a lovely lady, passed away in 2004 and I know she will be greatly missed by her family and friends.

On the many events that Phil and I participated in together, we organized ourselves so that I gave him access to my tender car. Usually after the event, I would meet Phil and Pauline in the bar for a drink and I would conveniently leave the car keys on the bar. Phil would pick them up and at the same time suggest that I take Pauline to the local bar down the road for one and that he would meet us there later. Phil would then go through the car taking any part that he wanted, lock up and then eventually meet up with us and surreptitiously return the keys to me.

On a couple of the occasions I had to fill in an insurance form as 'someone' had stolen the alloy wheels and tyres off the roof rack. How I got away with it I do not know, but I suspect the management had a fair idea of what was going on. This happened whenever Phil and I coincided on an event, so it was not difficult to work out the little plan that we had concocted together.

Alpine Rally

The Alpine Rally was my next event and, again, I prepared a recce car which was used by the navigators to check the route. The team travelled down to the south of France on the wagons-lits, the French railroad sleeping cars, from Boulogne to Avignon, which then left just a short drive to Marseilles.

This was my second visit to the south of France and it was on this trip that I came to the conclusion that whilst it was a very expensive area to be, I loved it. There just seemed to be something about the south of France that was right up my street: the atmosphere, the food, the wine and, of course, the climate were all perfect. As a team we always seemed work well and enjoy ourselves when we were in that region.

The event went reasonably well, although not as well as we had hoped after the success of the Monte. However, the company was satisfied with the results, which were acceptable. Pauline Mayman won the Ladies Cup, but Rauno was disappointed when a navigational error lost him the chance of gold, while Timo missed his coupé by 1.7 seconds. The Morley Brothers had fan belt trouble, which kept them down to second place in the GT class, but we achieved a 100% finish to win the manufacturer's team prize.

Testing in Wales

Johnny Evans and I spent a few weeks preparing, testing and modifying cars prior to the RAC rally. This was carried out at Strata Florida in Wales and, because of the distance from Abingdon, about a four-hour drive, we were put up in a delightful pub called the Vulcan Arms, in Rhayader, Mid Wales. This was a free house and I remember the beer and the food were both excellent. We spent a few days with the drivers, who were more than capable of wrecking a vehicle in a very short space of time on some of the tracks that we tested on. (See pictures.)

Most of the testing carried out was to see how the different types of sump shields held up under extreme conditions. The few weeks before an event was always a good time to put the suspension through these extreme situations to ensure that the hydrolastic units would stand the test with no ill effect on the suspension or body structure.

The units were manufactured especially for us and were fabricated from a harder compound rubber than the standard hydrolastic unit, which was made to offer the driver and the car's occupants a smoother and more comfortable ride. For production the standard unit was perfect, but it was not suitable for the rally cars, which had to contend with many different conditions and surfaces.

During the development of these units various increases were made to the hardness of the rubber diaphragm within, which would stiffen the suspension. We had to monitor the changes fastidiously as they could have had drastic effects on some of the other components. If the rubber diaphragm was too soft, the car would not handle very well over rough surfaces, and if too hard, severe damage to the front and rear sub frames and to the suspension could have been caused.

RAC Rally

The final race of the year was the RAC Rally. The Excelsior Hotel near London Airport had been the starting location for the last couple of years. We had a large entry of five Mini Cooper S, plus two Austin Healey 3000s. With the rally championship practically in the bag, Rauno, one of the flying Finns, only had to finish in the top five places for him to win the title.

Each year there were over 500 miles of special stages, and this year was no exception. The weather was atrocious as the convoy arrived in Wales and the conditions had become extremely wet. Paddy and Timo proved just how good the Minis were on the special stages and already showed on the leader board. Tony Fall, in a loaned works' Cooper S, was also in the top five.

After calling in at Oulton Park, which was a special stage on the race circuit, the route carried on into Yorkshire where the weather continued to deteriorate as the snow arrived with a vengeance. Near Hemsley there were about six inches of the white stuff. Stage 20 proved extremely difficult as the first few cars were traveling across virgin snows. This created numerous hazards and accidents as the drivers had great difficulty determining where the road started and finished. Several cars skidded about or swerved off the road, putting them out of action completely or delaying them slightly.

On the way to Pebbles in Scotland the Morley brothers crashed out of the rally. Timo, on the other hand, was flying now, mainly because the conditions suited him, coming from Finland. He led the rally with a gap of five minutes over Rauno who was lying second.

During this event, there was a service point at Pebbles where we stayed overnight. I shared a room with Roy

Brown at the Pebbles Hydro Hotel, which is now very famous for its spa. I'll never forget the receptionist asking me if I would like a hot bag in my bed, to which I replied that it depended on her name. She was very quick to reply that she was actually referring to a hot-water bottle.

During the night I was woken by an awful choking sound coming from the next bed. Very panicked but not wanting to let on, I asked if Roy if everything was OK and he explained, in an awfully hoarse voice, that he had partially swallowed his false teeth but had fortunately managed to retrieve them just in time. I reminded Roy of this event at the 2007 team reunion. Despite the fact that we both laughed about it, we also admitted that the incident had in fact scared the living daylights out of both of us.

In Perth, the poor weather brought the rally communications into chaos. Subsequently, the drivers were unaware of their positions, and Timo and Paul were surprised to learn that they were leading. Vic Elford, in a Ford, challenged Timo for second place. At Devil's Bridge Vic retired, and Rauno became the new lead challenger. On one particular stage, which was completely packed ice, the Timo's Healey, being a rear-wheel drive, lost traction. Quick off the mark, Rauno took advantage of the situation beating Timo by 49 seconds to take the lead, which he kept until the end.

We were all very happy for Rauno, yet also sad for Timo as both he and Paul had put in a tremendous effort. It was also a sad day for the Healey, which also failed to win the event after trying for so long.

Rauno's win gave him the European Championship for 1965 and this was a brilliant reflection on the car, Rauno and the team.

At the end of the year, the FIA published new "Appendix J" regulations with significant changes to the specification of the cars allowed to run in Groups I, II and III. For example, Group I was for cars built in minimum quantities of 5000 vehicles during the twelve months and with only minor modifications allowed.

Monte Carlo 1966

The first event under these new regulations was the Monte Carlo Rally and as the regulations were a bit ambiguous, Stuart Turner and the Ford Competition Manger flew to Paris to try and make sense of them with the Homologation Committee. In the end, no less than three versions of the regulations were issued before the start of the Monte, which caused the lads in the workshop a massive headache.

The management finally decided that our entry would consist of three Group I cars, a Group II for Raymond Baxter, and an MGB for Tony Fall.

The Group I cars had to run on 3.5x10-inch wheels, a 5.5-gallon fuel tank and a 4.1:1 final drive. The other modification of significance was the dipping system that we fitted to the headlamps. Two additional lamps were permitted in Group I, and we opted to fit two extra fog lamps using quartz iodine bulbs. To allow dipping of the main headlamps, you had two options by way of a three-way switch. The driver could either dip to the fog lamps or dip to the main beam, which fed the current through a resistor which would dim the main beam. It was also possible to have the fog lamps on separately to assist the driver on the special stages.

The details of the rally itself are not particularly exciting and it will suffice to say that the three Group I Minis performed perfectly, however, Tony Fall's MGB, unfortunately, retired with a broken oil cooler pipe.

In the dry, the Minis were beaten for speed by the Porsches and the Lotus Cortina, driven by Roger Clark, although Timo and Rauno were in the top five fastest cars on the last stage.

All this aside, it slowly became apparent during the event that the organizers had no intention of letting any other car win except for a French one.

In addition, the French press had a field day with their reports about the performance of the British Minis, seemingly amazed at how well they competed, and all sorts of rumours began to circulate about us cheating in some form or another.

The headlight system had not been a problem up until that point, but it then appeared that the organizers sought any reason they could for which to disqualify or discredit any car that finished in front of a French car.

At the end of the rally, the organizers provisionally

announced the winners, with the three Minis in first, second and third positions. Roger Clark finished in fourth in the Lotus Cortina.

After the event, however, well, the scrutinizers virtually stripped the three Minis and examined every single part of each vehicle. We also found out later that they did the same to the Ford, as they were determined to find something that did not comply with the regulations.

Nevertheless, when the results were announced, for a second time, the British contingent were appalled to see that their names had not been listed in the top four as before and that first place had instead been awarded to Paul Toivonen in a Citroën DS 21. (Later on in my career, when I worked for Citroën, I would have been delighted, but not at this point in time.) No reason was given for the judges' absence for over an hour, and then, when it was announced, they stated that the first four had been disqualified on a technicality relating to the headlights, which the judging panel said did not conform to the regulations in Appendix J.

An appeal was immediately submitted by Stuart Turner, along with Ford and Rootes, who had also had some of their cars disqualified as well.

Once again, the French press ran riot with their stories and suggestions of cheating by the British team. In order to try and resolve the situation, Stuart arranged a back-to-back test using a standard Mini Cooper S taken from the showroom of a local Monte Carlo dealer, who was more than happy to assist. Stuart invited the press to witness the event.

The ultimate result couldn't have turned out better as the drivers performed even quicker in the standard car than they did in the rally car. The publicity stunt was fully reported in the press the following day.

Still, in spite of this, the official appeal lodged by our team was thrown out by the organizers, placing the Citroen DS21 driven by Paul Toivonen as the winner, followed by two Lancias. In protest, Paul Toivonen decided to boycott the prize-giving, which, as you can imagine, didn't go down too well with those in charge. The prize-giving ceremony was always held in front of the Palace in Monte Carlo with the prizes being presented by His Royal Highness Prince Rainier.

After the whole sorry episode, the cars and some of the team were flown back to London Airport and welcomed by a reception committee that included the Mayor of Oxford, John Thornley (Managing Director of MG Car Company), and most of the wives and girlfriends of the team. Timo's Mini appeared on the London Palladium again, but this time the compere was Jimmy Tarbuck.

Despite the negative press in France, the general feeling was that the publicity received from the disqualification was far greater and far more rewarding than if we had been declared the winners, so, in actual fact, a lot of good came out of a bad situation.

Tulip Rally

As suggested by its name, the Tulip Rally began in Holland. I was selected to accompany Bob Whittington in one of the Austin Westminsters. This was always a pleasurable event due to the great weather usually experienced as the rally wound its way through Holland and Germany before finishing back in Holland again.

We only entered two cars in the Tulip Rally as it clashed with the Circuit of Ireland, where we also had interests. Rauno was supplied with a Mini Cooper S for his Group II car, and Timo also had one for his Group I race.

Unfortunately, my memory lets me down and my research on this event has not uncovered the information I hoped it would, but I can say that we had a brilliant result with Rauno winning and Timo finishing ninth overall, first in class and winning the manufacturers team prize. Bob Freeborough, a private entry, also made up part of the team.

Acropolis Experiences

Four years in succession the management selected me to go and accompany the drivers on the recce of the Acropolis Rally, which started in Athens. This entailed me driving a recce car, which was of the same specification as the event car, to Dover. At Dover I caught the ferry to Calais and drove to the Gare du Nord Station in the centre of Paris. From there, I caught the overnight sleeper to San Raphael in the south of France and then I drove to Marseille. At this point, I had to negotiate with one of the booking agents and try to successfully reserve a place on one of the passenger or cargo ships travelling to Patras in Greece for the car and myself at a sensible price.

This trip usually took three days and two nights and was generally a fun one. I remember one particular voyage in 1967 that was particularly pleasurable and sticks in my mind very vividly. (See Acropolis 1967.)

Acropolis Rally 1966

In mid-February I was given the task of building a car for Paddy to drive in the Acropolis Rally, with Ron Crellin elected as co-driver. The Acropolis always took place in late April or at the beginning of May and we were usually away for two weeks or one month if on the advance party.

I was given a brand new car straight from the production line which I had to completely strip to the bare body shell. I then rebuilt the vehicle as per the build sheet that management gave us and this outlined all the regulations for the proposed event.

In those days, a mechanic put together the complete car. The first task was to prepare the body shell as the regulations never affected the body fittings, meaning that little work had to be done there. We set about fitting all the hydrolastic fuel and brake pipes inside the car together with the hand brake cables. From there, we attached and connected all the components, which were either standard or had been specially checked by the manufacturer for the department, to the body shell. All the wiring harnesses were made individually for each car and inserted by two specialists from Lucas Racing and the Competition Department. The Group II cars were fitted with twin fuel tanks in the boot plus a twin fuel pump that could be changed over by the driver or navigator via a toggle switch on the facia.

Next, we undertook the task of building the rear sub-frame, which was completely re-welded and underwent one or two modifications. These included such things as additional skid plates on the lower members and special hydrolastic cylinders and bump stops to suit.

From there we moved onto the front sub-frame which, again, was re-welded. Several extra-strengthening plates were welded on in places that would not show when the engine and gearbox were subsequently fitted. The suspension units were assembled by carefully fitting special top and bottom ball joints. Once all this was in place, the units were attached to the sub-frame.

When it came to the engine, the first step was to draw all the parts from the Parts Department. Then, the cylinder block had to be bored out to increase engine capacity and the top face machined 0.010 inches above the level of the piston crown. This entailed partially building the engine and then stripping to machine the face of the cylinder block. Once the machining had been carried out, we set about a rigorous cleaning process of the block and oil ways. As soon as we were happy with our efforts we started to assemble the engine.

Firstly, we had to insert the crankshaft that had been specially balanced and onto which the pistons and connecting rods had all been fitted just before. We had to individually select and carefully weigh all the connecting rods because a Group I engine could not have any balancing or lightening carried out on it.
In order to overcome this, you had to take out all the con rods from stock and examine every single one until a matching set was found. It was essential that they were as light as possible, with both the small ends and big ends weighing the same. On a Group II engine, filing and polishing the rods was permitted.

After fitting the connecting rods to the crankshaft and tightening the big end bolts to the correct torque setting, we then had to measure the big end bolt to ensure that it had not stretched more than the permissible amount of .003 inches. Obviously if it had, then we needed to change it as it would have been considered faulty.

The combustion spaces had already been cleaned (or fettled as they called it) of all the casting imperfections at the foundry on the last stages of production by one of the engineering companies that we used. When we received the heads, the combustion spaces had already been polished as well. It was then a question of lapping in all the valves and assembling the head using specially tested valve springs.

The next component was the gearbox, which was completely stripped and the base of the casting machined to accept a full sump guard. It was then rebuilt using straight cut gears and by wire-locking all the selector locating screws and lock nuts, as these were a weakness and had been known to come loose on earlier events.

Once the gearbox was complete the engine could be fitted to it and the unit then fitted to the car. Finally, the remainder of the ancillary equipment was inserted and attached and once we got the vehicle running, it was necessary to clock up a few miles before letting it out onto the rolling road to establish the power curves.

After the huge job was completed and all the cars prepared and ready to go, the only task left was to select which mechanics to take to the event. In this instance, Tommy Wellman, Den Green, Bob Wittington, Brian Moylan, Roy Brown, Peter Bartram and myself were the chosen few.

On researching this event, I was reminded of an incident that Brian Moylan describes in his book (Works Rally Mechanic). Whenever we drove through Italy to Brindisi, we generally always collected tourist fuel vouchers at the border. These came in the form of coupons that were automatically handed back to the customs officer on leaving the country if we hadn't used them. All of this was the norm. On this one occasion, however, the customs officer on duty decided that we weren't tourists, and therefore weren't entitled to any vouchers. Although we never used to use them in any case, it was essential to have them to hand because we knew we would be asked to return them on the way out.

Well, at the docks, and our point of exit, the customs official refused to accept that we hadn't been given any fuel vouchers. This resulted in quite a long time arguing with the man, and all the while the dockers were waiting to load the cars onto the boat. We argued and argued and pleaded, but the official wouldn't budge. Brian suddenly decided to try another tactic and asked him how much money he wanted instead. As if by magic, the official's demeanour changed, for the better, I might add, and Brian was quickly ushered away into a small office. For many this would set off alarm bells, but Brian emerged a short while later having been offered a nice glass of wine while a few lira changed hands.

Anyway, back to the event, which was going exceptionally well for Paddy. He was fastest over most of the special stages and consequently went on to win the whole thing.

Unfortunately, another team was penalized for taking a short-cut and duly logged a protest about the fact that Paddy had received attention from the mechanics in a restricted area. As a result, Paddy was also penalized, which subsequently deprived him of his first place and relegated him down to third. This was a double blow because not only was Paddy robbed of his first place, but I would have been celebrating my first winning car had the result remained the same. Needless to say, the culprit was very apologetic and all was forgiven after a few drinks.

Alpine Rally

I was selected to go on the Alpine Rally, which was also known as the Coupe des Alpes, for a second time. The event started in Marseilles, passed through some of the famous mountain passes of the Alps and finished up back in the south of the country. This was always a tough event, not only on the cars, but also on the drivers and the mechanics as the weather was always very hot and humid. That year we stayed in a hotel in the Vieux Port region.

The company entered four Minis for Timo, Rauno, Paddy and Tony – all prepared to the latest specifications and the current regulations for the event at the time. Having built a recce car for the event, I was not involved in the preparation of the rally cars as well.

This year we fared pretty poorly as three of the four cars retired: Timo with engine problems, Paddy with a transmission fault and Tony Fall with a broken driveshaft. Rauno finished third overall and second in class behind an Alfa Romeo and a Lotus Cortina.

In September, it was announced that BMC and Jaguar Cars were to merge and that the company was to thereon be known as British Motor Holdings LTD, with the MG Car Company to be renamed as the MG Division of the new company.

The RAC Rally 1966

In 1966, the Sun Newspaper sponsored the RAC Rally and to lift the profile of the rally even higher, two Formula 1 drivers were recruited in the name of Jim Clark and Graham Hill.

Jim Clark had agreed to drive for Ford and Graham Hill was to drive a Mini Cooper S for us. Maxwell Boyd was Hill's co-driver on this occasion, and the car was to be the official entry for BBC Wheelbase and the Sunday Times.

In order to help Graham and train him up to perform as best as he possibly could at the rally, the company acquired a civilian permit to utilize the military testing ground at Bagshot and a day was organized to give Graham some experience of driving at speed over the typical surfaces that he would encounter on the various stages of the rally.

The company entered seven cars in this event, which, therefore, meant that the mechanics in the workshop had their hands full preparing these cars along with the one for Graham Hill. The drivers chosen for this rally were Timo, Rauno, Paddy, Tony Fall, Simo Lampinen, Harry Kallstrom and Majatta Aaltonen, Rauno's sister.

The RAC Rally was not the mechanics' favourite as it was usually wet and cold. More often than not it would snow in Wales and Scotland, which always put somewhat of a dampener on working on the cars at a service point.

By Stage 4 Timo was in the lead. As the route wound its way into Wales, Simo unfortunately rolled his car out of the rally. Graham's car developed a transmission problem in the West Country – something had come adrift in the differential and had pushed its way through the casing. This was patched up with plastic metal, but the car finally expired in the Lake District with gearbox trouble. I always felt that he was delighted to retire as he couldn't for the life of him understand how fast the top drivers raced over the terrain that the route took them and believed they were all totally mad.

At Aviemore, Timo had maintained his lead, with six minutes between him and Bengt Soderstrom, who was second in the Ford. On leaving Scotland after the overnight stop, following Timo and Soderstrom were Paddy in third position and Tony in fourth. Paddy broke a driveshaft in the dreaded Kielder Forest and dropped out of the rally. In the Yorkshire moors Timo retired with a blown engine after having achieved some of the fastest times. This left the Ford in an unassailable position with a fourteen-minute lead.

When the results were published, Bengt Soderstrom was declared the winner and we were placed in a very respectable second, fourth and fifth with Harry, Rauno and Tony respectively.

Stuart Turner Resigns

In January 1967, Stuart Turner announced that he was leaving the company to join Castrol Oil. He had simultaneously been offered a position at Ford Motor Company, which he turned down in preference to Castrol for ethical reasons. He didn't believe it was right to switch straight to our main rival.

Monte Carlo 1967

The general feeling in the company was that we should have boycotted the Monte this year, but the management decided that we would enter and with a 'let's show 'em' attitude instead.

In 1967, the organizers of the Monte Carlo Rally introduced a tyre handicap, which would obviously make things very interesting. The arrangement was that there would be two categories – one where you could use as many tyres as you could afford but with a 12% handicap, and the second in which you were limited to eight tyres per car over the two competitive sections of the event.

Stuart and the drivers decided that the 12% handicap was a little excessive and entered all the cars into the limited tyres category. This decision was not taken lightly due to the fact that an extra weight of another four wheels and tyres was a penalty on its own.

The wheels chosen for the event were Minilites, possibly the most successful competition wheels of the 60s and 70s. Ours, which were composed of magnesium alloy, were manufactured by Tech-Del Ltd. and came to us already homologated for the Group II cars. The weight saved over the standard wheels was 22lb and there was also the added bonus of the extra strength and greater efficiency in brake-cooling due to the design.

The next problem that we were faced with was where to carry the extra wheels as the Mini was never known for its boot capacity. We normally stowed two in the boot, but we had four to contend with and to secure two on a small roof rack would certainly have caused a massive wind restriction. We came up with the idea to carry them on the back seat, but for this Stuart had to obtain special permission from the FIA to do so. Once this was granted, we strapped the seat cushion to the back seat as it was not permitted to remove it from the car. In order to mount these wheels safely, the design office was asked to create a quick-release mechanism that would allow the occupants or the mechanics to remove the wheels with speed.

It was necessary to identify the cars that were in the limited tyre category, so the organizers decided that they should have a yellow patch instead of a white one for the numbers.

After all the publicity we received from the previous year's Monte, all the ancillary teams, such as Ferodo, Lucas, Dunlop and Castrol, were anxious to lend a hand and help in any way they could. The company, however, was very cautious on this one, as sometimes having too many people around at service points was a hindrance.

Five cars were entered into the competition, with two cars starting from Monte and one each from Athens, Lisbon and Dover. The drivers that year were Timo, Rauno, Paddy, Tony

Fall and Simo Lampinen, a very accomplished driver who often made up the numbers for us when we had a big entry.

As a matter of interest, Simo suffered from polio when he was younger and it had left him partially crippled, yet he managed to walk with the aid of two crutches. This did not in any way affect his driving skills, and he very often put in some very fast times.

All our cars arrived at Monte without incident, although Paddy had encountered a lot of snow on the run in from Athens.

Unfortunately, the road conditions were extremely dry, which was, in fact, not in our favour. We knew that the Minis could not match the speed of the Porsche driven by Klass, or the Lancia of Ove Anderson in these conditions. Vic Elford was driving the Porsche and we were under no illusion that we could ever keep up with him in the dry conditions.

On the first stage of the rally, the Minis were listed in the top ten fastest times, but by the second stage the Porsche was ahead of Timo and Paddy was in third.
When the Minis returned to Monte for the overnight stop, the interim results published showed Vic Elford in the Porsche leading, followed by the four Minis.

The next day, the fastest 60 cars lined up to complete the mountain circuit, but we knew that the first stage was dry so it was going to be tough on our cars. If only you knew how hard we prayed for snow that year.

On the Col de Turini, our prayers were answered and it started to snow. As a result, both Timo and Rauno recorded the fastest times. Timo beat the Lancia by 19 seconds and the Porsche came third. On the second time over the Turini Rauno was fastest. Unfortunately, a huge rock mysteriously rolled down the mountainside and crashed into the front of Timo's car damaging the oil cooler and the distributor. We all thought that it was sabotage, but there were no witnesses and the accident had taken place on a stretch of road that the spectators could not access. Klass's Porsche went off the road leaving Rauno with a small lead over the second Porsche driven by Vic Elford with one stage to go.

Electricity filled the atmosphere once again as the team, spectators and the press were itching to see if we could repeat the performance of the previous year.

The gods must have been on our side as it continued to snow and Rauno had a fabulous run finishing with a 13-second lead over the Lancia. The results were checked and published later in the day. Rauno did indeed win the event, Paddy was sixth, Tony Fall tenth and Simo fifteenth.

The scrutinizers were very thorough yet again, but went about their job with a totally different attitude to last year. They finally declared that the cars were all within the regulations. Just as well!

This was a brilliant start to the year, especially as it was to be Stuart's last Monte with the team.

San Remo Rally 1967

I seem to remember that this event clashed with the Swedish Rally so it was decided that Paddy and Tony would enter the San Remo and Rauno and Timo would go for the Swedish event. Rauno and Timo preferred the snowy conditions at the Swedish rally as it was what they were predominantly used to.

For the San Remo Rally, the supervisor gave me the task of building the event car that Paddy Hopkirk was to drive with Ron Crelling as his co-driver. When you build the car yourself, you always have a completely different outlook on an event, and this rally was no exception.

I was given a new Mini straight from the production line, which I completely stripped and then rebuilt according to the specification instructions I had been given.

My service crew traveling companions were Robin Vokins and the boss, Stuart Turner, and we made our way down in one of the Austin Princess Vandem Plas. Both Stuart and Robin were always good fun to travel with and there was never a dull moment as the three of us always got on very well.

Unfortunately, the snow had damaged numerous stages within the rally, many of which were impassable. Paddy was unable to complete his practicing session until just before the rally started.

During the early stages of the race, Paddy, in the Cooper S, lead and was closely followed by a Renault and a Lancia. However, by the halfway stage the Renault and Lancia had lost time and Paddy maintained his lead. The stages around Genoa were particularly rough and the Lancia eventually retired with a broken sump. On the other hand, whilst the Renault had won a couple of stages by a small margin, Paddy still held on to the lead. A mile from the end of the last stage, however, Paddy's drive shaft broke but with a bit of careful manoeuvring, he managed to limp to the end of the stage.

Stuart was never one for sticking to routines or schedules and it was often the case that if there was time, he would always opt to visit another service point if he could. This meant that we never really knew where we were going next when he was travelling with us. At this point in the rally, he decided that we should join Doug Watts at the last scheduled service point, although once there we realized that if we changed the drive shaft, Paddy would receive a time penalty as it would take too long. Paddy suggested that Doug should push him to the next control with the Vanden Plas. This was a bit of logical reasoning, but wasn't a legal action, yet it seemed to be the only course of action open to them.

With a significant amount of bumping they moved off. Paddy revved the engine and slipped the clutch to act out the scenario. The next time control was at the end of a steep hill and therefore Paddy was able to freewheel into it. He was also able to creep away again by slipping the clutch. When he was completely out of sight of the control, Doug fell into place behind the Mini and continued the pushing.

The final control was at the end of a tunnel. Doug managed to speed up to about 60 mph and just at the right moment backed off in order to allow Paddy to coast into the final control. Fortunately, the crowd, and the officials, were totally oblivious to the fact that there was a problem and sympathized with him when he suffered a complete clutch failure at the final moment.

When the final results were published Paddy had been placed in second position overall. What a result! The only person that thought something was amiss was John Davenport in the Lancia. He was actually quite upset and made a protest to contest these results. Nevertheless, despite his best efforts, the results remained the same and he had to settle for third place.

This event was to be Stuart's last with the team, and Peter Browning was set to take the helm from thereon.

Stuart's Farewell

In March, we arranged a farewell party for Stuart which was held at the MG Social Club and all our members of staff attended. Stuart was very respected by us all, not only for his organizational skills, his humour and personality, but above all for the perfectionism in everything he did, which he in turn expected back from his drivers and all the team.

Stuart was presented with a silver salver, a present from all the staff that we had all signed, along with a unique desk-set made by Corgi Toys and which contained miniatures of the four winning Monte Carlo Rally Minis.

We were extremely fortunate as Stuart was succeeded by Peter Browning, who just seemed to carry on where Stuart left off. Peter was a very experienced race organizer and time keeper and he already had knowledge of the department along with all the personnel. Most of us had read about his appointment in the Daily Express before the company announced it to the staff. We all admired Peter as we knew his background and knew he was a very capable person to succeed Stuart.

Stuart realized on the London to Sydney Rally, of which he formed part of the organising committee, just how much he missed the sport and shortly after this event he was made another offer by Ford, one that he could not resist.

Tulip Rally 1967

As usual, the rally started in Noordwijk, a lovely Dutch town situated on the coast. We always stayed at the Huis Ter Duin Hotel, which was a 5-star hotel right on the beach. This hotel was very old and big and all the rally crews stayed there as the location was perfect for the start of the race. It gave the impression that it was almost on top of the sand dunes but overlooked the town at the same time.

I was again selected to share a tender car with Bob, and this year we entered three Mini Cooper S for Timo, Rauno and

Julien Vernaeve, who made up the third member of the team. David Benzimra, the son of the BMC dealer in Nairobi, was loaned a car for this event, but unfortunately retired with a clutch failure towards the end of the rally.

On our first night in Holland while at one of our favourite restaurants, one of the waiters told us about a new café-bar that was opening in a few days' time and invited Bob and I to attend the opening party the following evening.

Bob and I arrived at the bar when the party was already in full swing. We joined in and chatted to a lot of people, who were all very interested in what we were doing. During the evening, Bob sat on a glass-topped table whilst deep in conversation. Suddenly, the glass broke and Bob fell crashing to the floor, luckily with no damage to his posterior. The table was not so lucky, however, as it smashed to the floor and lay in a thousand pieces. I later learned that maybe crashing to the floor on a glass table may not have been such a bad thing as Bob then recounted how he'd subsequently enjoyed it while a very pretty waitress checked his behind for any glass splinters that may have been evident.

The rally itself was a success, with Timo finishing in second place overall and first in class, and with Rauno third overall and second in class. Julien Vernaeve finished in the top ten, which gave us the manufacturer's team prize.

Acropolis Rally 1967

Once again, I was on the advance party for this rally and therefore travelled down to Marseille in the usual way. On this occasion, I secured the last berth available on a cargo ship going to Patras. The ship only had ten cabins and I think the reason mine was still available was because it was the most expensive cabin on board. It was great. There was an en-suite bathroom, air-conditioning, a double bed, a sofa, an armchair and a small table. It also looked to the outside and, being a double cabin, was nearly twice the size of all the other standard-sized ones.

Just after we set sail, I had words with the bursar and asked if there were any other English people on board. He said he would get back to me and later that afternoon informed me that there was only one other English person on the ship. He then suggested that I join the captain for dinner and he would arrange for me to sit with the other English person that evening at the Captain's table.

So, for the rest of the afternoon I explored the vessel which, being a cargo ship, only took me about ten minutes as there were many restricted areas that the passengers were not allowed to enter. There was, however, a small area of the deck just below the bridge that had been converted into a sundeck and was reserved for the passengers. Only the bar staff on board were permitted to enter this area. After making a few enquiries, I was invited on to the bridge, and the captain, who spoke perfect English, gave me a very detailed explanation of all the equipment there. By the end of this little visit, I felt that the captain and I had become friends.

At 8.30 p.m. we all assembled in the bar for cocktails before entering the dining room, where we were all warmly greeted by the captain. It was then that I noticed a very shy-looking young lady around the age of 20. Well, you can imagine my delight when the bursar introduced me to Carol, the only other British person on board the ship. She certainly stood out, anyway, as she was about 5ft 6" with brown hair and dark eyes. She had a nice full figure and was extremely attractive; her prettiness accentuated by the short miniskirt she wore which showed off her extremely shapely legs that seemed to go on forever. Carol was very well-spoken and had obviously come from very good stock. (Shame she had to meet up with me.)

It turned out that she was, in fact, 24 years old and a nanny. She was returning to a family in Athens after having been on a three-week vacation with her family in the UK.

Once again I was in the right place at the right time. During the evening, having the pleasure of sitting at the Captain's table, we were able to enjoy some excellent French wine – the captain's choice – along with some very special brandy. I wasted no time in getting to know Carol, who also appeared extremely interested in me too with all the questions she was asking. In actual fact, it turned out that Carol was not as shy as she looked.

The captain was anxious to practise his English and as there were only the two of us that spoke the language, he spent the entire time talking to Carol and I. He questioned us about where we came from, what we did, and where and why we were going to Greece. This, of course, saved us both a lot of time asking one another the same questions later. At some point during the meal, the captain also explained to all those present that a rough storm was brewing and there was a strong possibility that it would hit us around 3 a.m.

After dinner, the captain invited us both to his lounge where we sat and continued the conversation. When we eventually escaped, we went for a quick walk around the deck to clear our heads a bit, but it was a little windy so we didn't stay out too long and returned to our cabins after a short while.

We parted with a kiss on the cheek and knowing exactly which cabin the other was in. As it happened, she was in the cabin directly opposite mine.

It was about 2.30 a.m. when I was awakened by a tremendous clap of thunder and felt the swell of the sea affecting the movement of the boat. My immediate thoughts shot to the mechanics of the vessel and I wondered whether the boat was fitted with stabilizers. This I doubted very much as it was a fairly old boat. The swell worsened and around 3.15 a.m. there was a knock on my door. I shouted that it was not locked and, to my surprise, Carol walked in looking very distressed (I think).

She asked me if she could stay with me until the storm subsided as she was terrified of the storm and hated thunder and lightning. Before I could open my mouth, she suddenly burst into tears. I quickly jumped out of bed and rushed over to console her, completely forgetting that I was in my birthday suit. Being a gentleman, I quickly wrapped a towel around me and proceeded to comfort her. We talked for a while and then she shot into the bathroom and threw up. By the time she came out, I had returned to the warmth of my bed, so I suggested that she got in with me, which she did only on the condition that I put some clothes on. I agreed.

However, when she threw up, some of the sick had landed on her nightie, so I suggested that she take it off and changed into one of my T-shirts instead. She agreed and on removing her clothes, I was gobsmacked to see that she had the most perfect figure – slim, nicely shaped hips, trim waist and perfect breasts, not too big but nicely formed. As she lay next to me, however, she made it quite clear that I was not allowed to touch her in any way other than to console or cuddle her. Well now, how was I supposed to interpret that remark?

Suddenly, another clap of thunder made her jump and ultimately snuggle up to me. The thunder carried on for another hour and, I have to admit, that every time she snuggled up to me, I got hornier and hornier. This then made me wonder how long it would be before I got a slap, as I was sure she could feel my John Thomas pressing into her back. It is difficult to believe that I behaved almost like a perfect gentlemen for the whole night, and, you're right, I did take advantage and let my hands accidently stray a bit each time she snuggled into me.

We both eventually fell asleep and woke at about 8.30 a.m. By this time, the storm had subsided and I offered Carol the use of my shower rather than have to walk down the corridor to the ladies' shower room from a cabin that wasn't her own. She gladly agreed and afterwards we made our way down to breakfast at around 9.30 a.m.

Many of the other passengers looked a bit rough as a result of the storm. Needless to say, you can imagine their faces when we entered the breakfast room together. We joked about the storm and I teased her saying that she wasn't really afraid of thunder at all; she just wanted to get into my bed. She teased me back about how I had jumped out of bed naked. I asked Carol if she approved of what she had seen and she replied telling me that it had felt more than adequate from what she remembered of the digging in her back during the night. She also added that it's not what you have, it's the way that you use it, which I thought was a very promising or kind remark.

We spent the morning sunbathing on deck and I couldn't let the opportunity of us both rubbing suntan lotion into each other's backs go amiss. She did give me a playful smack when I suggested she turn over so I could do her front.

We enjoyed a nice buffet lunch at around 2 p.m. accompanied, of course, by a tasty glass of wine. Due to the fact that we'd undergone an interrupted night's sleep, I suggested that we took a siesta, which she thought was a very good idea. Just before we arrived at her cabin, I took her hand and led her into mine, explaining that mine was more spacious and had air-conditioning, which fortunately for me, her room did not.

She did not object one bit and we spent the rest of the afternoon snuggled up on my bed. However, we did not get the sleep that I thought we might. Instead, we spent the whole afternoon seducing each other. She might have only been 24 but she taught me moves that I had not experienced before.

The rest of the voyage was either spent on deck sunbathing, in my cabin or in the dining room. Each evening the captain would invite us to join him, which was always appreciated as he supplied some excellent wine and some of the best brandies I have ever tasted. Even better was the fact that my bar bill at the end of the voyage was negligible.

We eventually arrived at Patras, disembarked and passed through customs. Rather annoyingly, one of the customs officials insisted that the carné I had for all the parts I was carrying was not acceptable unless it was in Greek, and not in the English, French, German or Italian that it was actually written in, which, in normal circumstances, would have been acceptable. So I then had to rapidly find a translator who could do a technical translation for me there and then. Surprisingly, there was someone available and I was taken aside to an office and introduced to a man who said he would do the translation for me.

On completion of the necessary documentation, I returned with the translator to the customs house where I was immediately granted entry. I eventually found out to my expense that the translator was brother of the customs official who had originally refused me entry. This set me back about six hours and around £100, but I was cleared quite quickly. I continued the three-hour journey to Athens and made my way to the hotel where I was staying at Glyfada Beach.

The hotel was stunning. Well, it wasn't a hotel in the traditional style, it actually consisted of beach bungalows positioned at regular intervals around the shore. The beauty of it was that you could wake up in the morning, order your breakfast from room service, walk 20 metres to the sea, have a swim and as soon as you saw the waiter coming in your direction, you got out of the sea and returned to your chalet. Each chalet had a bedroom, kitchenette and en-suite bathroom plus all the other features of a five-star hotel.

Once we were settled in, Carol spent a lot of her free time, including several evenings, with me until the rest of the team arrived, which was when, of course, I had to share a bungalow with one of my colleagues instead.

On the first day I reported to the B.L. distributor in Athens and contacted the drivers, who then filled me in on all the troubles that they were experiencing with the cars. I then had to relay this information back to the UK so that we could make the necessary modifications to the event cars that were being shipped out a couple of weeks later. I spent my time during the day with the drivers, who invited me to dine with them in the evening when I was not otherwise engaged.

At the weekends, if Carol was free we would take a trip to the countryside for the day and then go back to the chalet in the evening for a swim and dinner.

One weekend, we drove out into the countryside doing the old tourist bit, came across a beautiful little Greek village and had lunch in a small taverna that all the locals used. The lunch consisted of Greek salad and roast lamb and was to die for. Later on, we unfortunately had to leave and make our way back to Athens.

However, on the way back, whilst driving down through all the hairpin roads, the car suddenly skidded on the gravel at the side of the road, rolled over the edge and landed on its roof. Once we had gathered our thoughts, we realized that we were upside down. I somehow managed to open my door and, as I was about to scramble out, I noticed the 100-foot drop next to us. I calmly explained to a frantic Carol that the only way out was through her door as there was very little to support us on my side. After about ten minutes of struggling we managed to get her door open.

As soon as we had escaped and collapsed safely on the other side of the car, we looked down and saw where the car had come to rest. Breathing a sigh of relief, we realized at that point exactly how extremely lucky we were not to have been hurt and to be able to tell this story today. The car was upside down on its roof about 20 feet down, perched perilously on a cart track with nothing on one side and a sheer rock face on the other.

We flagged down a local tractor driver and he helped us

secure some ropes onto the car and winch it out. When we rolled the car over, the damage to the roof was quite extensive and I wondered how I was going to talk my way out of this one.

We were still able to drive the car back to the hotel and I remember sitting in a traffic jam heading into Athens when a driver alongside of me shouted over that the car didn't appear to be the same shape as it had been that morning. Apparently, he and his mates had spotted my car, which was almost in full rally trim as we drove out of town first thing.

That evening, we had dinner and an early night as we were both exhausted after our very eventful day.

When the drivers eventually saw the car and I explained what had happened, they offered to carry the can for me, but I had already spoken to my contact at the main dealers and he had organized for it to be repaired before the boss arrived in a couple of days' time.

The night before the rally started, the officials invited all the teams to a cocktail party on the roof garden on top of the Kings Garden Hotel. It was a great night and we met many old friends, but, like all these functions, it was a bit stuffy so we all decided to leave quite early and stop off at one or two of the many bars that we knew on the way back to our hotel.

The group returned to the hotel at about 2 a.m. in the morning and Johnny, who was sharing with John, clumsily knocked a bottle of drink onto the floor as he was preparing for bed. John jumped out of bed to help clear up and unfortunately stepped on a piece of broken glass, cutting his foot quite badly. The following morning Bill was detailed to take the patient to the local hospital for treatment, and once there the doctor proceeded to poke around the wound for any glass that might have been left stuck in his foot.

John spent the next five days traveling around Greece with me in the tender car in discomfort and he obviously could not get around very well as his foot was very painful. He was also convinced that there was still something in it. Nevertheless, John was very dedicated member of the team and despite his injury, which was causing him a great deal of pain, made sure that he did not let the team down and assisted me in every way possible.

Unfortunately, he was unable to drive so I had to drive from service point to service point, grabbing a nap here and there wherever I could. I was beginning to feel extremely tired and my energy was rapidly deteriorating, but, like John, I had to keep going. Whenever we arrived at our service area, John urged me to rest while he set up.

The wound was very reluctant to heal and when John finally attended a hospital in the UK, the doctor removed quite a large piece of glass from his foot, after which the wound healed very quickly.

The rally went extremely well for Paddy, but Rauno and Henry were not so lucky as they were involved in a head-on accident when they met another vehicle travelling the opposite way on one of the stages. This resulted in them both being sent to hospital too, fortunately not seriously injured, though.

Timo was lying second to Paddy at the halfway stage and was followed by the Lancias and the Ford Lotus, but the rough conditions were taking their toll and Timo arrived at the service point with a broken sub-frame. We quickly tipped the car onto its side, welded the frame together and sent Timo on his way, but unfortunately he arrived at the next service point with a broken gearbox.

After eleven stages Paddy led the race, with only a driving test followed by a hill climb and a race at Tatoi to complete. On the hill climb Paddy was the fastest, but in the final race his oil pressure dropped dramatically and he had to slow right down just before the finish line to ensure that he was able to complete the final lap and win the event.

With Paddy Hopkirk having been declared the overall winner of the event, this meant that we had a very lively prize-giving party that went on until the early hours of the morning.

Peter Browning had arranged for some of the party to be flown home, but the main group, which included a couple of the navigators and their partners, returned to the UK via the Greek liner Chania at Piraeus. (The previous name of liner, which had been painted over, was the Warwick Castle.)

During our stay in Athens we had collected and been given a

huge amount of beer and Greek wine that was contained in these decorative wicker-covered flagons, so we decided to take it all on board with us for the journey home. When we arrived alongside the boat and began to carry these flagons of wine on board, we heard the other passengers commenting to each other that we must be bringing our own water on board.

The cars entered the ship via an opening in the side of the hull and had to drive up some very crude planks of wood that had been strategically positioned from the dock side to the opening. When they drove one of the Vanden Plas onto the planks, the driver revved it a bit too much. This spun out one of the planks and the car dropped on to its chassis. The car weighed a tonne as it had been loaded with all the parts, but the crew eventually manhandled the car so they could reposition the plank and drove the vehicle on board.

Well, it wasn't long before we found out that this boat was in the last three days of a mini-cruise. The passengers, who were mostly German and American, all seemed fed up to the back teeth by this point as they had had no real entertainment on board throughout the trip. On hearing this, we immediately thought that this would provide us with the perfect opportunity to let our hair down and keep the celebrations going.

On our first night, the entertainment officer organized a Mr and Miss Ship contest and asked us all to get involved. Obligingly, we all agreed to take part and at the same time try to liven the boat up a bit. So we grabbed a partner from the other passengers and briefed them on our plan, which they all seemed very willing to comply with as they had been bored out of their skins for the previous seven days of the cruise.

A colleague of mine and I roped in a couple of American girls, both around 25 years old, and the other guys organized their partners as well. The evening commenced with a drink together which we all shared in the biggest cabin that we had amongst us. We'd previously stored the wine and beer in the bath to keep it cool. It was unfortunate, however, that every time there was a bit of swell the bottles would roll and clink together, which did not help the occupants of the berth who were trying to sleep.

Well, after a hilarious evening, Bill and his partner Liz were finally declared the winners of the competition. To round off the night I ended up walking around the deck with the American girl before heading down to the cabin with the alcohol in the bath to enjoy a quiet drink together.

Once again I had chosen well, as she had a fabulous sense of humour, was very attractive and had a very shapely figure that I would have loved to explore. Unfortunately, she was having none of it. As I was sharing with one of my colleagues, we re-joined the rest of the team and passengers back at the bar at around 1 a.m. There were still plenty of people there as no one wanted to go to bed in case they missed something. We shared a nightcap together and, as you can imagine, I took a lot of ribbing from my colleagues about my prior whereabouts, which I took, never letting on that we had spent most of the time on deck.

On the second night, the entertainment officer organized a dance, which also went down quite well. All the lads joined in the fun and got most of the passengers involved, who seemed to enjoy themselves immensely too.

When the liner finally docked in Venice, many of the passengers thanked us for making the last couple of days of their cruise thoroughly enjoyable.

Once all the cars were off the boat, we drove to Milan in convoy where we caught the night sleeper to Boulogne, the cross-channel ferry back to home soil and eventually drove back to the works at Abingdon.

Austrian Rally School

During the summer of 1967, BMC Austria coordinated a training course for the future up-and-coming Austrian rally drivers and other interested parties. This was held on the roads and forest tracks of a military training area about 75 km from Vienna.

Bill and I were selected to attend and, with the aid of a trailer, we took a Mini Cooper S with us to assist Rauno and Paddy, who were to be the instructors on the course and were flying direct to Vienna.

On the first night in Vienna, Paddy, Rauno, Bill and I stayed in the Vienna Hilton in the centre of the city. Recalling it now, it was one of the most magnificent hotels that I have ever been fortunate enough to stay in. After a superb dinner and some fine wine and brandy, which we were glad BMC Austria were picking up the tab for, we eventually gave in and went to bed.

The next day, we drove to the military testing ground which was set in a stunning location surrounded by pine trees and mountains. We were quite happy to stay in this idyllic setting, which was lucky as we were due to stay for three nights. The quarters were a little sparse compared with the Hilton and the meal arrangements were self-service, but excellent nonetheless.

Paddy and Rauno completed a few demonstration runs with each driver, who then put into practice what they had learnt in their own cars. Some of the drivers were quite good, but when they were given the opportunity to drive a simulated stage against the clock, one or two were a little too eager to prove their capabilities and at least two cars ended up badly damaged, fortunately without injury. By the end of the course, there were three or four bent cars that had been damaged over the three days.

It was, however, one of the most relaxing trips that I had been on as no one was up against the clock at any point and there was no pressure of any kind. Staying at the Vienna Hilton, which was absolutely fabulous, was the icing on the cake for me on this particular trip.

Alpine Rally

The Alpine was becoming one of my favourite events as the weather was always great in the south of France and I was beginning to love the French way of life, not forgetting, of course, the food and the wine.

This year, the management decided to enter three Group VI Minis for Timo, Rauno and Paddy, a Group II Mini for Tony Fall, and an Austin 1800 for Brian Culcheth.

With the Group VI cars we were allowed to reduce the weight wherever possible without it having a detrimental effect on the strength of the body shell. Aluminium panels were fitted to the doors, bonnet and boot lid along with Perspex windows to all the doors. The specification changed dramatically when dealing with the Group II cars and entailed considerable more work.

On the first stage from Marseilles to Alpe d'Huez, which was around 1,400 km at very fast pace, several retirements were brought about. This included Rauno with a broken gearbox. Tony Fall was also involved in an accident on the stage, which actually ended his rally. At the completion of this first stage, Timo was third behind two very fast Renault Alpines, and Paddy was lying in seventh place. Brian was leading his class in the 1800, an extremely big car to throw about these mountain passes.

The second stage was about 700 km and played heavily on the brakes. As you can imagine, there were several more retirees. Timo was still third and Paddy was now in fourth place, but at the service point it was panic stations as they both had to contend with brake problems. Timo had to be fitted with new calipers again, along with new tyres, and Paddy with a new brake servo, brake pads and tyres. Brian only required new pads and tyres.

The final stage was 1,600 km long. Timo suffered a broken throttle cable and with insufficient time to change it, he jammed the throttle partially open and drove for the next two hours on the ignition switch. Both the Alpines retired on this stage. On the higher section of the stage a thick fog hung in the air. Nevertheless, Timo and Paddy took advantage of this and set the fastest times. Unfortunately, on the descent of the Col d'Allos, Timo retired with an idler gear-bearing failure.

At the finish, Paddy had managed to hold his lead and was declared the winner. Brian in the 1800 enjoyed a well-deserved class win.

My first born

I digress for a moment as 1967 was a very special year for me. On 13 September 1967, my eldest son, Andrew, was born. He was just perfect in every single way and we developed a very close relationship from a very early age due to the fact that his mother suffered from post-natal depression.

RAC Rally

Each year, the final event was always the RAC of Great

Britain. It was decided this year to enter a Group VI Austin Healey 3000 together with a Mini Cooper S for Timo, with Group II cars for Paddy and Tony Fall. With all the cars prepared and about three days prior to the start of the event, the organizers announced that it was to be cancelled due to a recent outbreak of foot-and-mouth disease. This was great news for me as it meant that I could spend more time with Andrew.

Monte Carlo Rally 1968

We always prayed for snow on this event as the Minis were exceptionally quick with the drivers we had, but if it was dry, it was difficult for them to compete with the Porsches and the Renault Alpines. The cold and snowy conditions were not particularly pleasant for the mechanics to work in, but a good result always made up for it and the difficulties encountered.

Four cars were built in the Competitions Department for Timo, Rauno, Paddy and Tony, and three cars were built by Special Tuning: an 1800 for Brian Culcheth, along with two cars for BMC Publicity.

When our crews arrived in Monte, we stayed at the Hotel du Helder, a super hotel which we were all familiar with as over the years if we were in that area, the company always booked us in there. The location was perfect as it was right in the middle of the city with only a short walk to the nightlife and it was on the main highway going through the city centre.

On the run into Monte all the cars arrived without incident, although one or two had experienced heavy snow on their journeys.

During the previous few months we had been experimenting with the Weber carburettors and after the cars had arrived in Monte, Peter Browning was called to the organizers' office for a discussion on their fitting because the scrutinizers believed that they did not meet the regulations.

Peter was all for pulling out of the rally, but after long discussions with the drivers and Longbridge it was decided to complete the event.

At the start of the mountain circuit, which consisted of six stages, we were lying fourth, fifth and seventh. During these six stages, there were no less than 21 service points covering the route with most of the mechanics tending to the cars at least three times during the night.

Timo was the only casualty when the car suffered with overheating problems, but the dry conditions on this event had favoured the Porsches and the Alpines.

When the results were published Rauno was placed third, Tony fourth and Paddy fifth behind the Porsches, with Brian in the 1800 in 24th place and second in class, along with winning the touring category and the team prize. This was another fantastic result.

The program this particular year was a bit light, but there was some very prestigious events during the year which made up for it.

East African Safari Rally 1968

This was the first time that we had entered a team in this rally and it was unfortunately a very disappointing result for all involved. All the 1800s retired early and we had hoped and expected to finish the event in the top 10 with at least a first in class, but that was not to be. The safari was usually held in April with a route that took you through Kenya, Tanzania and Uganda. It had been started by President Kenyatta outside the Nairobi City Hall.

Extensive testing was carried out at the military testing ground at Bagshot and we discovered many weaknesses in the body shell, suspension tube and housing which were strengthened accordingly. This rally was a very gruelling event and really punished the suspension, so it was necessary to try to get it right when we were building the cars.

The team left Gatwick in the afternoon and as they had been enjoying a good run, the publicity department had arranged a huge send-off with all the media. The company had hired a Britannia aircraft to fly the team and the cars to Nairobi.

The day had started off with a buffet lunch in the VIP lounge at Gatwick Airport, with the odd drink here and there. There were a lot of photographs being taken of the cars being loaded with the drivers and then of the whole team together. Once we were on board the aircraft the party continued as only we knew how. Fortunately, the captain and his crew did not object to us having a bit of fun, which meant that the three hostesses were run of their feet serving drinks to the 14 of us on board for the whole of the ten-hour journey. They were tickled pink with the songs we were singing and even joined in with a few numbers as they did not get many flights as relaxed as this one. Nevertheless, I think deep down whilst they enjoyed it, they were quite shocked with the variety of our songs.

On arrival at Nairobi we were taken to an apartment block just off the Kenyatta Avenue, which was one of the busiest areas of the city. This seemed to be the district where all the main hotels were situated and where, we were told, all the aristocracy lived.

We were to spend our next four weeks here except when we were on the rally. I shared an apartment with two of my colleagues and we had our own house boy, who was in his thirties, to look after us. Every day he prepared a full English breakfast, which always went down a treat, did our washing and ironing and kept the apartment spotless. He was a real gem. When we finally left the apartment, the three of us gave the boy the equivalent of £100 as a tip and, bless him, he burst into tears. We found out later that this was the equivalent of three months' salary – which fully explained his reaction.

My colleagues were great fun to share with and the three of

us got on like a house on fire, getting up to all kinds of mischief.

Most evenings we would go to one of the big hotels for dinner as they usually had some form of entertainment on. Then after dinner we would go down to the nearest nightclub. Every time we rocked up to the entrance, the doorman was always very reluctant to let us in because we would have been the only white people in the club. After about the third time there, however, he started to greet us like we were old buddies.

I seem to remember it was on this rally that I really got the taste for French brandy and drank copious amounts each night. Doug, one of the supervisors, had introduced me to it several years previously when he and I were on the Monte together. Doug and I got on so well he was almost a second father to me.

I remember going out one evening to a dinner-dance in one of the larger hotels and one of my colleagues got involved with this English lady. I can only describe her as being about 26, very pretty, with long hair, blue eyes and the most curvaceously full figure, which was shown off by her low-cut figure-hugging dress that just about contained her boobs and left nothing to the imagination.

Anyhow, as the night went on we all had lots to drink and I remember turning in before the rest of them as I was beginning to feel the effects of all the brandy I'd drunk.

About two hours later, I heard the door open and I could

hear a lot of giggling. My pal and this girl, who, by the way, was a presenter with the BBC in Nairobi, entered the room. I pretended to be asleep and they proceeded to get undressed and got into bed. From the groaning noises they were making, I guessed that they were obviously enjoying a very close encounter.

I then heard a lot of whispering and to my amazement felt the bed cover being drawn back. The next moment I realised that she was next to me in the bed. Well, I was not quite ready for this beautiful creature, but it didn't take her long to raise my desires to a new level and, strangely enough, it didn't take her too long to reach her peak either. This girl knew how to enjoy herself, what she liked and exactly how to get it.

After she had finished with me, she got back into bed with my colleague and promptly made love for the third time. But it wasn't all over with just yet as she then invited us both to get into bed with her, which we obviously did as we did not want to disappoint the young lady.

All the mechanics spent many a long hour on final preparations during the first week of our stay at the BMC dealer Ben Bros in Nairobi. We were allocated a section of their very large open-air workshop, which we all loved. As the recce cars came back in each night we inspected them and any serious defects would be noted and amended within the rules of Homologation. We always made sure that the modifications could not be seen by the naked eye and, therefore, not create any suspicion from the Homologation scrutinizers who would examine the cars at the start and finish of the event.

Both Timo Makinen and Tony Fall had not driven in the Safari before, but both thought they had a good chance of doing well. Rauno Aaltonen and Henry Liddon had competed in it four times but had never finished.

The rally got underway at the beginning of our second week and the three cars were doing well until the second night when Timo went out with a fractured oil cooler.

Tony Fall and Lofty Drew's car had trouble with the alloy housing that supported the top suspension arm, which was duly replaced. Unfortunately, they were outside of the maximum lateness permitted and were therefore disqualified. This fault was annoying as it did not show up in the recce cars during practice.

Rauno also suffered the same problem when he was lying third and we replaced the housing, but this was also carried out outside of the permitted time limit.

Now this left us with a problem as all the cars were out of the rally and the Britannia aircraft was not due to return until the end of the month, which was 11 days away. So, over dinner that night, the team discussed what to do and it was decided that we would take a trip to Mombasa on the Indian Ocean. Four of the team decided to travel by train and four of us decided to drive as we felt it would give us the opportunity to see a bit more of the country.

The route from Nairobi to Mombasa on the A109 skirted the Chyulu Hills National Park and went right through the middle of the Tsavo National Park Game Reserves and the towns of Tsavo and Mangu.

Tsavo is one of the biggest game reserves in Africa, covering some 21,000 sq. km, and is divided into two halves that make the East and West National Parks. It is particularly famous for its elephants. Most of the park is almost completely closed to the public and is the home to the largest herds of elephants in Kenya, along with all the other wildlife. There had been lots of reports of how the elephants had attacked visiting tourists by ramming their cars and we were advised not to stop under any circumstances if we came across a herd of these creatures.

Well, you got it, we did come across a herd of elephants that were quite close to the road and we promptly stopped to take photographs of these enormous beasts.

I remember Mike, who was driving at the time, sitting on the roof of the hire car to get a more enhanced view than the rest of us. We were all out of the car taking pictures when suddenly the bull turned towards us, making a horrendous noise and flapping its ears. We carried on taking photos, totally oblivious of the danger we were in, when suddenly he started to charge the car.

Well, I was the first to get back in, but it took a few precious seconds for Mike to get off the roof and for the others to ensconce themselves back into the safety of our vehicle. From my position as first back in, I could immediately see this enormous elephant getting nearer and nearer. I was at my wits end and didn't know whether to stay in the car or make a run for it. If the elephant were to make contact with the car, it would have been my side that he hit, and I did not fancy these big tusks coming through my door.

Mike finally got the car, a Peugeot 306, going and we sped off with all the doors open and Mike doing 0-60 mph in about five seconds. This must surely have set a new world record for both Peugeot and the Guinness Book of Records.

That night at the hotel in Mombasa, we were regaling the others with our story when a waiter handed us a newspaper that was about a week old. In it was an article that described a similar incident that had happened the previous week. Unfortunately, the occupants of the car had not been so lucky as the elephant had turned the car over several times and damaged it so much that the four people, who remained inside the vehicle the whole time, all lost their lives. You can imagine how lucky we all felt.

The local dealer in Mombasa was originally from Hertfordshire. He kept us well-entertained and threw us a party on the second day with lots of good food, drink and pretty girls, all of which were appreciated. Needless to say, a great time was had by all. I remember that the dealer had two very attractive daughters around 23 and 25 whom he was very protective of. He was determined that they should keep their knickers on at all times, especially as he had probably heard that we had been away for a couple of weeks and all our hormones were running amuck. However, the girls were just as determined that their knickers were coming off, so a colleague and I decided that we should not disappoint them and assist whenever possible.

Well, the old man did not let them out of his sight all evening, but we craftily managed to arrange to meet the girls later that night at around midnight on the beach in front of our hotel. When the party broke up, my pal and I went back to the hotel and dressed appropriately for the beach. We sat under the palm tree that the girls had chosen at the given time, and waited. It got to ten minutes past midnight and we became convinced that they had stood us up. Suddenly, and to our surprise, the two sisters appeared out of the sea – completely naked.

We walked about 200 m in the sand to a secluded area where the girls had left all their belongings, together with blankets, bottles of wine and pieces of chicken, which, I must say, went down extremely well at that time of night. After the initial pleasantries, we got stuck in and these two girls taught us both a lot that evening; things that I had never imagined were possible.

The following day I guessed that their father must have caught wind of something as our boss told us to stay away and not meet up with them again. But, alas, my brains were now in my trousers and we met them again that night at a predetermined rendezvous that we had arranged the evening before. That predetermined spot was actually my bedroom, if I remember rightly. We continued with the lesson from the night before.

All in all, the whole trip was superb. We gained an awful lot of experience in more ways than one, which we hoped would stand us all in good stead if the company decided to enter again the following year. We sincerely hoped that would be the case.

Tulip Rally 1968

I had only been home for a couple of weeks and then I was selected once more to attend the Tulip Rally in Holland.

Only two cars were entered on this occasion, one for Timo and another for Julien Vernaeve. Julien was to later on become a very good friend, and I am pleased to say that we still often exchange emails.

On the first stage, which was on the Zolder circuit in Belgium, the Fords and Renault Alpines were much faster than the Minis because the tarmac condition suited them better. Both the drivers suggested that the cars were down on power, and at the overnight stop we paid particular attention to the timing to try and improve on the performance.

Timo suffered a rear-wheel puncture twelve kilometres from the end of the stage and finished that part with the alloy wheel welded to the brake drum. This was easily overcome by fitting a new brake drum and wheel. On the next stage, Timo made a rare mistake and went off the road through a hedge and came to rest on soft ground. There were not many spectators around, so they walked to the end of the stage to let the marshals know they were OK and then went back to the car.

By the time they had returned to the vehicle, a small gathering of spectators had surrounded it. Paul gave the rally plates to a couple of people in the crowd and then a group of them manhandled the car back on the road, which enabled them to finish the stage. They convinced the marshals that the rally plates had been stolen and they stamped their time card accordingly. Paul was adamant that they could make the next control on time, so they proceeded on to the next check point. They made it with seconds to spare, despite having been delayed for so long on the stage with their mishap.

Timo made some very quick times over the next few stages and Julien, who had been tussling with a BMW, ended up first in the Group II class and third overall. Timo was 41st out of 44 finishers and, despite the poor result, it was very important to the team to have all cars finish to ensure that we won the team prize.

A Three-Month Interlude

I had just returned from a two-week holiday with my family in Dawlish Warren when all the mechanics in Competitions were called together to discuss a problem that had developed on production. At that time, our department was not so busy, and the company was looking for two volunteers for this job, which necessitated a temporary transfer to the Rectification Department for three months to help out with the production problem.

Apparently, a batch of engines had been sent to the factory from the Engines Division in Coventry, and it was suspected that they all had porous cylinder blocks, meaning that it would be necessary to replace all the engines.

Things had gone a bit quiet in the department and there were lots of rumours that the company directors were going to cut the rally programme. I decided to volunteer along with Derek Plummer. Derek was the same age as me and we had spent a lot of time together during our apprenticeship.

We both handed over the cars that we were preparing at the time and reported to Charlie Rosin, one of the foreman in Rectification who we both knew very well. We had worked under him for six months during our apprenticeship. As soon as he clapped eyes on us two this time around, Charlie's opening words to us were: "What the hell have I done to deserve you two?" He promptly informed us that there were 145 MGBs in the compound that required new engines. He also told us that we could undertake the task any way we wanted to but the maximum time allowed to carry out the replacement was nine hours per vehicle.

After we had sorted out our work bays Derek and I moved the first car in. Despite all the suggestions of how we should carry out the job, we appraised the task together and decided on the quickest way to carry out the replacement. We actually worked on the first car together too so that we could discuss the order of what items needed to be removed and then confirm our plan of action.

Firstly, we agreed to remove the bonnet, radiator, complete

with the mounting panel, and the oil cooler but leave the pipes connected and tie them up out of the way. Next was to disconnect the engine mountings, fit an engine sling and disconnect all the electrics and controls in the engine bay.

We then removed the gear lever as we believed it would be quicker to remove the engine and the gearbox together rather than disconnect the gearbox and leave it in situ. The last thing was to take the weight off the engine on the sling and to remove the gearbox support member. The only thing left then was to hoist the engine out with a block and tackle, swop the gearbox and clutch assembly over to the new engine and reverse the whole operation.

By the time we had completed two replacements, we were down to a time of just four and a half to five hours per engine. So, this meant that between us we managed about four engines a day. With a couple of hours overtime two or three days a week, the whole job took us just under three months. Some days felt a bit monotonous, but luckily the characters that we worked with ensured that we never got that bored.

The author aged 7 in the school uniform of Carswell Primary School

Machu Picchu

The author and his first car purchased from his brother

The author's parents' wedding day 12th December 1935

The author's parents at John and Betty's Wedding day

The author's grandparents

Three of the rowing crew from the Maidenhead Regatta with two of the coxes. Why there are only three of us I do not know.

Doug Watts presenting Stuart Turner with his fair well gift from all the Technical Staff March 1967

All the Apprentices at a Christmas function in 1961.
Front row L/R Peter Bartlett, Brian Purbrick, Roger Newbold, John Dunbar, My Brother Bill, Robin Vokins, Cyril Carter, Keith (spud) Faulkner, The Author, Michael Legg.
Back row, a visiting apprentice from New Zealand, Michael Dicken, Bob Staniland, John Yaxley, Bernard Stimpson, Geoff Clark, Terry Ward, Peter Bartram and Michael Clewley

157

Testing to destruction in Wales, both the Mini and the MGB had the same treatment on the Welsh terrain

Loading the Britannia for Niarobi

The author carrying out roadside repairs on the way back to the factory after testing in Wales

159

The author's eldest son Andrew and his lovely wife Karen

The author's youngest son Matthew with his lovely partner Heidi

Presentation night at the golf club. L-R The author, John Gordon a good friend and one of the trophy winners, Steve Jones Secretary of the P.G.A.

The author in action in Spain. Don´t look too closely at the waist line. This must be the worst golf swing I have seen, whatever happened to the straight left arm?

One of the functions we attended at the British Embassy in Nairobe a couple of days before the start of the East African Safari. From the left, Roy Brown being served, two of the Dunlop tyre specialists, the author, Mick Hogan and Fred Pearce

The three 1800s Land Crabs as they became known) ready to be shipped to Nairobi via the Britannia

Paddy Hopkirk and the author, discussing the car that I had prepared for him at the end of the San Remo Rally of the Flowers

Timo Makinen - one of the Flying Finns as they later became known

The girls going strong in the Beauty Box on the World Cup Rally

One of the triumph 2.5 Pi`s undergoing some major repairs at one of the service points

Another Triumph 2.5 Pi going strong, showing the rough terrain of many of the special stages in South America

Andrew Cowan and crew going well at this point in the event on tarmac in the author's car

Brian Moylan at the border control trying to convince the officials that our papers were correct as described in an earlier chapter

John Rhodes in action at Brands Hatch for the opening race of the Saloon Car Championship

Rally Cross at Lyden Hill Kent with the Morris 1100 and the Cooper S in action for the Saturday afternoon viewers of BBC Sports World

Paddy Hopkirk and Ron Crellin on the 1967 Monte Carlo Rally carrying the extra tyres as per the regulations described earlier

The return to the department

We returned to the Competitions Department at the end of November and immediately got involved in the rally cross programme that had been devised for BBC television during the winter months. The annual dinner and dance for the department, which was usually a tremendous night, was causing a problem because over the same weekend there was a rally cross meeting at Croft in the North Country and they were looking for two volunteers to support the event.

As Derek and I had been out of the department for nearly three months we decided to go to Croft and miss the annual bash. As it turned out, the weather was appalling that weekend and we experienced great difficulties travelling up on the Friday as it had begun to snow and the travel conditions were deteriorating rapidly. We immediately realized at that stage that what lay ahead was a very cold, wet and muddy race meeting.

We took two Mini Cooper S on trailers for John Rhodes and John Handley, who we met at the hotel quite late at night as the travelling had taken us much longer than we had imagined.

The event went reasonably well but it was as we expected – extremely cold and also muddy as the snow had started to thaw on the Saturday morning. However, at the end of the event we ended up with John Rhodes in third and the other John sixth overall. I remember when Derek and I had finished packing everything away and had loaded the cars back onto the trailers, we hosed each other off to remove the mud that we had collected on our waterproofs.

The merger

At the end of 1968 news came of the British Leyland merger and we all wondered what the future held for the Competitions Department. Lord Stokes was to head the company and he had already closed down the Triumph Competition Department. However, it was decided that the department at Abingdon would remain, although the programme for the coming year was greatly reduced.

1969 Programme

The rally cross programme continued every Saturday afternoon over the winter months as it created a lot of interest and publicity being a televised event. We prepared numerous cars for these shows, including Minis, a Triumph 1300, a Morris 1300 and a Rover 3500. The two venues for this programme were Lydden Hill in Canterbury and Croft in the North.

We used various drivers including Paddy Hopkirk, Brian Culcheth, John Rhodes, John Handley and Geoff Mabbs. Between them, their efforts brought the company even more positive feedback from the publicity that we gained from each race meeting, not to mention the fact that the shows made extremely good viewing for the television public as well.

It had been announced earlier that the rally programme was to be reduced and we would concentrate on saloon-car racing, utilizing different production cars, predominately the Cooper S, and introduce other cars as the year went on.

Brands Hatch

My first race meeting was the opening meeting of the Saloon Car Championship at Brands Hatch. We entered two Minis which were to be driven by John Rhodes and John Handley, two very experienced saloon car drivers.

We had to carry out a lot of trying and testing with different carburettors, fuel injection systems, 10 and 12-inch wheels with knock-on wheel hubs and different engine specifications, to name just a minority of what we had to contend with.

The first race meeting did not go well in more ways than one. I accompanied Bill in the transporter with the two cars on board. We left the workshop at around 4 p.m. to travel to Kent, anticipating that we would arrive at the hotel between 7 p.m. and 8 p.m. just in time to join the rest of the team for dinner.

However, on the hill heading out of Henley-on-Thames, we suffered a total clutch failure, which left us totally stranded halfway up the hill. After several calls to the factory, which had closed by this time, we eventually secured the delivery of a long wheelbase flatbed lorry along with a Sherpa van. We loaded the two cars onto the flatbed and secured all the gear inside the van. Eventually, a huge tow truck arrived to recover the transport. By now, it was almost 9 p.m. so we decided to have a meal in Henley and stay the night there.

We arranged with the hotel to leave around 6 a.m. so that we could be at the circuit by 9 a.m. As it was a Saturday morning, there was no traffic about and we arrived half an hour early in the pouring rain.

Things only got worse. At the start of the first race, John Rhodes was involved in a start-line accident and completely wrote off the car. This put him out of both of the races as the first race was run in two heats. Then, in the second heat, the other John got caught on the grass, spinning a rear wheel off it and creating a lot of damage. That was the end of his race.

So, our first race meeting was a complete disaster for a manufacturer's team. And it just seemed to continue because as Bill was about to leave the circuit with the flatbed lorry, he got stuck in the mud and had to be towed out by one of the Brands Hatch tractors.

Silverstone

The second event in the championship was the Daily Express International Trophy meeting at Silverstone. Once again the two Johns drove for us. Two more cars were hastily built and although neither car had been tried or tested, they finished fourth and fifth. It became very evident at Silverstone that the Escorts were much faster and would become a problem for us as they were going to take some beating.

All the mechanics found it very difficult to adapt to the atmosphere of a race meeting, and even more difficult to come away from a meeting without the results expected by the directors of Leyland Cars. On reflection, I realize that I found it virtually impossible to switch from the rally environment to that of the racing world in such a short space of time. Nevertheless, we knew that we could all build a very competitive car.

Hockenheim Circuit

My third meeting took place in Europe at the beginning of June 1969 at the famous Hockenheim Circuit in Germany. We were hoping to put on a good show for the European market with a couple of Minis. This event was for Group II cars, which were almost standard cars with the exception of modifications to the engine, carburettors and front shock absorbers, all of which had to have been homologated previously. With a Group II car you were not allowed to remove things like bumpers, heaters or the full trim that was fitted on production.

A lot of testing was carried out at Silverstone and Thruxton in an endeavour to be more competitive with the Ford Escorts and to correct some of the problems we had experienced at previous meetings. Firstly, we tested an engine with a shorter stroke which was producing 131 BHP at 7000 rpm, and the exhaust was changed to a long, open pipe, which gave the engine a further pull of 150 rpm down the hanger straight. After 21 laps of the circuit, the crankshaft broke, so it was back to the drawing board.

Two days later, we prepared the car for testing again, this time at Thruxton as the Silverstone circuit was not available. After adjustments to the suspension and shock absorbers, John Rhodes was finally happy with the car.

We took the cars to Hockenheim in the transporter with no problems this time; that was until we arrived at the circuit where we then discovered that the transporter was not able to fit through the tunnel that led to the paddock.

The weather was extremely hot and, as expected, the cars were overheating in the first practice session. So, for the second session, we removed the thermostats and fitted blanking inserts. We opened up all the radiator grill slats on the front of the car to allow more air in and turned the heater in the car to full heat. This reduced the temperature by some 15 degrees.

During the race, the Alfa Romeos were proving too fast for the Minis, but John Rhodes managed to slipstream one of them and put in some very heroic driving, which the crowd loved. We finished third and fourth in class, which was very respectable after some great entertainment from the two drivers.

That evening, we dined at our hotel and the staff laid on several jugs of ice-cold white wine, which went down rather well as it had been a very hot day. We finished with fresh strawberries and cream, which also went down very well. As you can imagine, being looked after like this made us very reluctant to leave the hotel.

European Six-Hour Race

The next meeting was at Brands Hatch at the end of June for the European Six-Hour Touring Car Race. I was not involved in this event as I had been asked to prepare a Mini Cooper S for Paddy to drive in the Tour de France.

However, two cars were entered and were to be crewed by John Rhodes/Paddy Hopkirk and John Handley/Roger Enever. The two cars finished second and third in their class. The company was very happy with this result as it was our first long-distance race.

Mallory Park

At Mallory Park for the 4000 Guineas meeting, John Handley experienced our first retirement from a mechanical failure when a piston malfunctioned. John Rhodes went on to finish fourth overall. Again, I was not involved in this race, nor the following two endurance races, or in any of the preparation.

Nurburgring Six-Hour Race

The endurance races were quite important to the company

as a lot of publicity could be gained from these events. The mechanics who attended this event had their work cut out as both engines had to be removed after practice in order to attend to clutch problems. This work was carried out through the night in the pit bays of the paddock. Unfortunately, both cars retired with broken trailing arm pivot shafts, which was a huge disappointment as they were first and second in their class.

Spa 24 Hour

Again, two Minis were prepared for this race. However, just before it started it began to rain. Well, it was actually a torrential downpour. It took about six laps for the track to dry out, which caused one or two problems with the choice of tyres. John Rhodes' car retired with a collapsed valve seat, and the other car continued at speed. However, after 255 laps of some very competitive racing, it threw a con rod through the crankcase.

Tour de France 1969

The management decided to enter three Mini Cooper S for this event for Paddy, John Handley and Brian Culcheth. Julien Vernaeve also entered his own Group I car with the full support of the team.

I was instructed to build Paddy's car, and it was decided that it would be fitted with a fuel injection engine. John Handley's car was to have Weber carburettors.

A considerable amount of testing was carried out at Silverstone in order for the drivers to get used to their cars and iron out any problems. We opted for the Minilite wheels with knock-on wheel nuts. These were great and easy to change at service points or pit stops.

The boss wanted to get some more miles out of the ex-Scottish rally car – a Triumph 2.5 PI – and utilize it on the tour as a service car for himself, Bill Price as driver and myself as riding mechanic.

This event, which started in Nice, was extremely gruelling for both the cars and the team. It covered some 5,000 miles over eight days in September, so the weather was still very warm, and included ten race circuits such as Spa, Nurburgring, Le Mans and Clemont-Ferrand, to name but a few. There were also 11 hill climbs involved.

The first section included several of them and the Minis performed well with John Handley leading Paddy by two minutes. Julien was leading Brian in the Group I class, which Brian was extremely unhappy about.

On our way to Nurburgring, the gearbox on the Triumph 2.5 started to get very noisy, so I persuaded Peter to stop so that I could check it. It was very low in oil, but as I didn't have a syringe with me, I couldn't top it up through the filler plug. The only option I had was to remove the cover along with an inhibitor switch and, with the aid of a tea pot we had in the canteen, I was able to refill the gearbox with oil.

At Clemont-Ferrand Paddy started to suffer from an oil

surge and had to make a pit stop for a top up. After the race at Rheims, John and Paddy were going well and were fourth and fifth overall respectively, with John being some five minutes up on Paddy after having to make the pit stop. Paddy had more trouble at Albi when a heater pipe cracked, but fortunately I was able to cut the cracked portion of the pipe out and, utilizing a rubber hose and jubilee clips, was able to reconnect it. Unfortunately he lost more time from this pit stop, but no damage appeared to the engine from the overheating.

However, later that day, Paddy started to lose power and with a long road section ahead we had time to investigate. On taking off the rocker cover, we found a broken valve spring, but we did not have time to remove the cylinder head to change it. So, by removing a spark plug from the offending cylinder and using a screwdriver bent at right angles, I was able to support the valve whilst a colleague replaced the broken spring. The whole operation took about 15 minutes. With the long road section Paddy was able to make this time up without losing any more.

At Nogaro, the Minis had the crowd on their feet, as Brian was actually leading the race whilst Paddy had to stop to change a plug. Nevertheless, within six laps Paddy had worked his way up to third overall behind one of the V8 Camaros and Brian's Mini. Paddy then suffered a puncture, yet from being in last position, he stormed through the field to overtake the remaining competitors before the end of the race.

When the results were published, Brian's great drive had

not been good enough to beat Julien in the Group I class, and they finished first and second. Paddy finished fourteenth overall and first in the Group II class.

Paddy was awarded a Pewter Tankard for his class win, which he presented to me, and I am pleased to say that I still have it today.

RAC Rally

As usual, the year finished with the RAC rally, which in 1969 had sponsorship problems. Again, I was not involved with the preparation of the cars, but as always the whole team was out on the event, which was an extremely cold one. The rally started at the Central Airport Hotel near Heathrow. Three Triumph 2.5 PIs were entered and it was pointed out by our press officer that this was the first event that we had entered a team of non-BMC cars. This didn't matter as this rally was to be used as a good test ground for the forthcoming World Cup Rally.

On the special stages the Triumphs were not that competitive with some of the other cars, but a battle was developing with a team of Datsun for the manufacturer's team prize.

When the cars moved into Northumberland, snow and ice caused huge problems on the special stages and the rear-wheel drive cars received a lot of help from the spectators as they ran out of traction.

At the halfway stage, the only complaint from the drivers was that the shock absorbers were too soft on the Triumphs, although no major repairs were necessary, which was very encouraging.

When the rally restarted and moved into North Wales, there was a lot of heavy snow and one of the stages was cancelled as a result. To help cope with the conditions, the Triumphs were supplied with snow chains and were fitted on several occasions.

Andrew Cowan managed to put his car off the road and was helped back by willing spectators. Paddy's car suffered gearbox problems and the local dealer was more than willing to let us use his workshop to change the gearbox. Because the control was in complete chaos, we decided to take advantage of this and moved the car into the dealership and started to change the gearbox. It was going to be touch and go as to whether we could get the car finished before Paddy had to check out of the control area. However, Tony Nash, the navigator, was taken to the control and he managed to check out without presenting the car which was most unusual, but it gave us the time to finish the job.

The team battle continued between Datsun and us, but unfortunately Brian lost some time when he encountered fuel injection problems which allowed Datsun to take the team award.

The next few months were taken up with testing and preparing the cars for the forthcoming World Cup Rally.

World Cup Rally Experiences London – Mexico 1970

In 1970, the World Cup Football Tournament was to be held in Mexico and the final at the Aztec Stadium in Mexico City. Our rally organizers planned it so that every country that was represented in the tournament would be visited during the event.

All the major manufacturers entered teams of cars and our entry (British Leyland) had entered seven in total, all with dual sponsorship. The Triumph 2.5 PI to be driven by Andrew Cowan, Brian Coyle and Uldarico Ossio and the Triumph 2.5 PIs to be driven by Brian Culcheth and Johnston Syer, Paddy Hopkirk and Tony Nash were sponsored by the Football Association. The Mini Clubman to be driven by John Handley and Paul Easter was sponsored by BBC Grandstand, the Austin Maxi driven by Rosemary Smith, Alice Watson and G. Derolland was sponsored by the Evening Standard. Another Austin Maxi driven by the Red Arrow was sponsored by Autocar. The Triumph 2.5 PI driven by Evan Green and Jack Murray and accompanied by Hamish Carno from the Motor Magazine, who also sponsored the car.

I was more than happy when the boss asked me to prepare a Triumph 2.5 PI for the World Cup Rally to be driven by Andrew Cowan. Andrew, of course, won the London to Sydney Marathon in 1968, so I was very pleased to be preparing a car for someone that had had such experience.

Because the event was being run over eight weeks and covered some 16,000 miles, a lot of which was over quite rough terrain, we carried out, as you can imagine, a great deal of testing. Much of it took place in South America in hire cars and we also utilized the MOD rough-circuit testing ground at Bagshot for the Triumph 2.5 PIs. This was a very useful testing ground as it was only a couple of hours away from the workshop. If any problems occurred during these tests, it was possible to implement any modification necessary and retest again. We could also modify the rally cars as they were being prepared in the workshop.

From the recce in South America we realized that the terrain was very rough in places and that the drivers would have to negotiate quite deep water on several occasions. It became obvious that the body shell would have to be strengthened and be watertight. It was arranged for Press Steel Fisher to build special bodies incorporating an aluminium roll-over bar, additional welding to all the seams, flared wheel arches and vents in the front wings, not to mention aluminium panels for the doors, bonnet and boot, an air intake in the roof along with six extra jacking points.

Some of the other modifications carried out to the Triumphs included Perspex side and rear windows, Koni shock absorbers to the front and rear, special stub axles with Triumph Stag front brake discs and rear drum brakes.

The standard fuel tank is 14 gallons and this was increased to 32 gallons by fitting two supplementary tanks, a 10-gallon tank on the left side and an eight-gallon tank to the right side of the boot space. These tanks were made of a special lightweight reinforced canvas and neoprene. This necessitated having two high pressure fuel pumps fitted with twin Bendix transfer pumps in order to pump the fuel from the side tanks to the master tank, which overcame the fuel injection problems. Both these pumps were operated from a toggle switch on the facia within reach of both driver and navigator.

The co-driver's seat was totally modified to convert into a full-length bed with special seat cushions and seatbelt. All the seats were fitted with sheepskin covers. Fifteen x 5.5-inch Minilite wheels were fitted with Dunlop SR Sport tyres and twin spare wheels were fitted to the centre of the boot compartment between the fuel tanks, and modified boot lids provided the extra space to accommodate them.

With regards to the engine, a specially tested cylinder block with a finely balanced and crack-tested crankshaft along with a TR6 camshaft and a Jan speed exhaust manifold, which produced 150 BHP were added. The gearbox was fitted with Triumph Stag close ratio gears with overdrive and this operated in conjunction with 3.7:1 final drive with the Salisbury Powr-Lok differential.

As always, a Halda twinmaster was installed to aid navigation along with an altimeter as the drivers were concerned about the effects of the high altitudes that they were going to encounter when crossing the Andes. To counteract this we also fitted a carrier to place the oxygen bottles which would be installed at the appropriate time. The only other modification that I can remember was the alternating air horns provided by Maserati.

On top of all these modifications the car was completely stripped on arrival and painstakingly put back together with kid gloves incorporating all the above items, utilizing nylock nuts where possible.

I really enjoyed preparing this car, which probably took me about ten weeks, possibly more so than any other I had prepared and I was extremely proud when I had completed it and saw Andrew on the start line with MY car.

I cannot comment on the modifications of the other models that we entered as I was not involved in their preparation, but they were all very similar and we made ourselves aware of what was going on, on a daily basis.

Counting up the days to the event and our traveling time meant that we were to spend three weeks in Europe followed by seven weeks in South America. This was to be one of the longest trips that I was fortunate to be a part of.

The rally started at Wembley Stadium by the England team captain Bobby Moore, with the European leg passing through Munich, Vienna, Budapest, Belgrade, Sofia and finishing in Lisbon. The drivers found this leg relatively easy. The only problems experienced were in Yugoslavia and this was due to a bridge closure that caused major delays. From my point of view, the leg was very straightforward with no problems at any of the service points. At the end of this leg, Brian Culcheth lay in sixth position, Paddy in eighth and Andrew eleventh overall.

At Lisbon the cars were shipped to Rio de Janeiro on the Royal Mail Ship 'Derwent'. This enabled all the drivers and their crews to relax for about ten days before they started the South American leg, which they all knew was going to be very tough on both cars and drivers.

The company had chartered a Britannia aircraft from Caledonian Airways for this event and for at the end of the European section; all the team converged on Lisbon where we had an overnight stop for a de-briefing session.

The following day we flew to Buenos Aires calling in on Dakar in Senegal where I remember we had to disembark whilst the plane was refuelled. I can visualize the toilets in the airport now, as they were the most disgusting I have ever come across in my life. People had done their business in the toilet, on the floor, out of the cubicle, in the passageway and out of the door to the toilets. We were all totally gobsmacked by the horrendous smell, together with the awful sight of it all and could not believe people did that sort of thing.

We had to land again in Recife, Brazil, for refuelling and finally arrived in Buenos Aires at 2 a.m. on 28 April 1970. We stayed at the Hotel Gloria in the centre of the city for a few days while we acclimatized to the temperature, which was about 35 degrees. It was also extremely humid, which meant that we spent many hours by the pool, which, fortunately for us, had its own bar.

The night before we left Buenos Aires we were all invited to attend a reception at the British Embassy which was hosted by Sir David and Lady Hunt. The event was for all the British teams and meant that we all had to put on our best frocks.

The rally restarted on 8 May. Three days prior to this, we, the support team, left Buenos Aires in the Britannia to be dropped off at our appropriate locations in order to prepare our first service point.

My first port of call was in Montevideo in Uruguay, and, as I remember, Tom and I were one the first two to be dropped off. This is where we encountered our first problem in South America, which had some dramatic results and cost me dearly in gratuities, or bribes – call them what you like.

When we arrived at Montevideo airport it was about 12.30 a.m. We had already been warned that the airport closed at midnight. After circling the area, the pilot called Tommy and I to the cockpit and explained that the airport was closed and he could not alert anyone in the control tower.

He then explained that he could land the plane on his landing lights, but it would mean that we would have to jump from the aircraft. This meant that we would be entering the country illegally. The main problem was that the pilot had a very tight schedule and if he did not land then, he would not have time to return with us after dropping the others off. It was decision time for Tom and I. We agreed that work came first and told him to land and we would accept the consequences.

He made his final approach, put the landing lights on and brought the Britannia in perfectly. However, as soon as he touched down he brought it to a dramatic stop. The hostess opened the door and laid some steps out, but they did not touch the ground. Our gear was thrown out onto the runway and Tommy and I were being encouraged to follow via the steps.

Well, I don't know how many of you have looked down from an aircraft and realized how far you are from the ground, but my first thoughts were I wonder what the hospitals are like here because if I do not break a leg doing this, I never will.

I did not have the luxury of thinking about it as the hostess assisted my exit to a huge roar from my colleagues. I landed on my suitcase, which broke my fall, and the suitcase. As I looked round, I could just make out the Britannia taking off again and my immediate thoughts were, "Oh shit, was this really the right decision? What have we done?"

I looked around me to see where the nearest buildings were and decided it was so dark it was anybody's guess as to which direction we should struggle towards with all the gear we had. Then suddenly the decision was taken out of our hands and we did not have to worry anymore as in the distance we saw blue flashing lights. We knew instantly that this was where the fun and our problems were going to start. We also realized that we could not have gone very far as it would have been impossible to have carried all the gear they had thrown out with us.

A very old Land Rover pulled up alongside us and we were unceremoniously put into the back of the vehicle together with all our belongings and the boxes of parts that we were carrying with us. They drove us to the airport buildings and we were ushered in between two very big, dark-skinned, black-haired security guards with very thick arms and extremely shabby uniforms.

A senior officer, who was much shorter than his security guards, dressed in an immaculate uniform topped off with a hat with lots of gold braid around the peek, which he kept on all the time, was waiting for us. He had a pencil-thin moustache, was dark-haired and had very big teeth, not to mention a very big stomach. He immediately gave us the impression he was very important and the one that we really had to convince that we were not going to be a problem to. He was waiting for us in his office, which was in the main terminal, so that he could interview us individually.

This proved very difficult as he conducted the interview in Spanish and, at the time, neither of us spoke any Spanish. Consequently, we did not understand much, so obviously didn't answer many of his questions. Whilst we were being questioned, the remainder of the security team thoroughly searched our luggage and the boxes of parts for anything suspicious. When we analysed things later, the one thing we both thought extremely strange was that they did not carry out a body search on either of us.

The guy in charge ordered us to be taken to the cells where we were left to our own devices. Mobile phones were not available in those days and neither of us were given the opportunity to use a landline, so we just had to sit it out until morning in two separate cells.

It was planned that an interpreter would meet us when we

landed, so we both knew that we would not be forgotten and would have someone to help us at some point. We also knew we would have to wait till morning, providing the authorities allowed him or her to see us. At least my cell was dry and warm – perhaps a bit too warm compared with the UK, but beggars couldn't be choosers and I decided to get as much sleep as I could.

Apparently the pilot had explained to the boss on board the Britannia exactly what would happen to us – that we would be arrested and detained for at least one night, after which hopefully it would be sorted out with a big bribe to the guy in charge. These comments obviously made it easier for me when I submitted my expenses forms some two months later.

Anyhow, at about 7.30 a.m. my cell door opened and a guy came in and introduced himself as our interpreter, José. He was about 6 feet tall and around 45 years old, quite slim with a big mop of hair. He spoke English perfectly and had a good sense of humour.

He asked if I had any money with me and I explained that I had about 2,000 US dollars on me, which was a lot of money in the 70s. I actually had closer to 4,000 USD, but I did not want to give all my secrets away as I did not know if there was a limit as to how much you were allowed to bring into the country. I had this feeling that I was just about to part with a lot of money to get out of jail. I remember thinking at that point that situations like this were when you could really do with one of those get-out-of-jail-free cards from the Monopoly board game.

He took the 2,000 dollars and vanished, returning to my cell about ten minutes later, and said: "Ok, we go." I had this strange feeling that there was no point in me asking for a receipt. To this day I do not know if all the money was passed on to the guy in charge or if the interpreter pocketed some as well, but I did not get any change and wondered how I would word this one on the expense sheet.

The two security guards that had arrested us the night before were strangely being exceptionally helpful and friendly carrying all our belongings and escorting Tom and I out to the waiting car of our interpreter. At the time I thought to myself that hopefully this was the biggest tip I have to give or am likely to give, but at the same time I realized that in South America money talks. I also wondered whether there would be any repercussions when we came to leave the country in ten days' time.

Well, thankfully, at the time of writing this book, this is the only experience of jail that I have encountered so far in my life and hopefully it will end up having been the only one.

From the airport we drove across town to the Intercontinental Hotel, which was on the seafront and built like a palace. Despite being a day later than planned, the hotel staff greeted us with open arms. The hotel itself was very luxurious and we enjoyed the comforts and our time there immensely.

The first thing we did was take a shower and as we had not eaten for about 12 hours we then sat down to a hearty breakfast and discussed our plans for the next few days. Fortunately, the jail incident had not delayed us too much and as Tom and I were to go our own separate ways, meeting up again a few days later, I asked the interpreter to drive me to the location of my first service area, which was about an hour and a half away, to see what facilities were available there and to set about hiring staff for the event. I needed at least two good mechanics to assist me.

At the service area there was a very big lay-by which I decided would be ideal, but I was also worried about keeping all the gear I would have around me, such as wheels and tyres, which I am sure would have had a good street value over there, secure. I pictured having to hire a dozen security guards to keep it all together, although, in our favour, there seemed to be very few modern cars about that these tyres would fit anyway.

I was amazed to see so many Model T Fords driving around and later learnt that there was a factory in Montevideo which still made these cars and produced spare parts for them some 50 odd years after they went out of production at the Ford Motor Company in America.

I was discussing my thoughts with my interpreter when I noticed a big yard next to the lay-by which I decided to have a closer look at. I approached the gate and was greeted by two huge German Shepherds that didn't appear to be very friendly at all. From the look of them, they weren't regularly fed.

I told my interpreter that I wanted to use the yard and

whether we could find out who owned it and then arrange a deal with him to hire it for the day without the dogs. I was shocked and surprised that we got away with only having to pay $100 US dollars, which I was happy with as it gave us complete privacy and security, which was my main concern.

Once we had got everything organized, we were able to relax by the pool and take it easy for a couple of days before the rally came through town. That evening, the interpreter took me out to dinner at a BBQ restaurant and I had the biggest Argentinean T-bone steak I have ever seen, which was cooked to perfection, medium to rare, with blood still oozing from it on the plate.

He also informed me that he had organized for me to appear on television later that evening to be interviewed with another interpreter for a programme that was the equivalent of the Uruguayan 10 O'clock News.

Well, as it turned out, the interpreter was a very pretty young lady of about 25 called Anna. She was around 5ft 6" in height, dark-haired, with a beautiful complexion and a perfect figure. She asked me what the purpose of my stay was and what part I was playing in the rally. I have to explain at this stage that the studio we were in was about 75 sq. m and the news desk was at one end and I sat alongside the newsreader with the interpreter next to me. The rest of the room was packed like sardines with people who presumably had come in off the streets. In my vain way, I thought they wanted to catch a glimpse of me.

I was extremely nervous but answered all the questions that

were fired at me without any difficulties and Anna interpreted them to the camera and the audience. I thought the interview was over and that it had gone extremely well, but then the newsreader suddenly turned to me and asked Anna a question which made the audience gasp. She then turned to me and asked if it was correct that I had been arrested the previous evening when I landed for possessing cannabis.

I duly explained that yes, I had been arrested, but not for possessing cannabis, but for illegal entry into the country as the airport was closed when my plane arrived. I went on to explain that because of the tight schedule that the plane was on, there was no time for it to return the following day. When I think about it now, I wonder how the security staff to whom I think I had given $2,000 USD got on and how they had explained it to their superiors when they had heard my tale on their 10 O'clock News.

Well, on leaving the studio, I was the obviously the celebrity of the night and I was flooded with offers of marriage, autographs and young ladies wanting to celebrate the night with me. Anyhow, as we were leaving the studio I spotted the interpreter Anna and went over to ask her back to the hotel for a drink. She replied that she would be delighted to and would meet me in the foyer in about an hour.

This was perfect as it gave me the time to take a shower, change my clothes and wait for her as arranged. When she arrived she had also changed her clothes and wore a tight-fitting dress that hugged her body and accentuated all her curves perfectly. We sat and talked for a while over a couple of drinks and then she said that she had only ever been in the foyer of the hotel and that she was very interested in seeing the rest of the hotel and would it be possible for her to see my room. Well, I nearly fell out of the armchair I was in, thinking all my birthdays had come at once when she suggested that. So, I first showed her the dining room, which had a large dome in the centre that was filled with a huge chandelier, obviously the centrepiece of the room. This room opened up to another big conference room and theatre. From there we made our way to the lift and went up as far as the tenth floor, which my room was on. Then I gave her another conducted tour, showing her what both room and the occupant had to offer.

Well, after taking breakfast in the room the following morning Anna said she had to be at work at 9.15 a.m. so we arranged to meet that that afternoon for a swim in the pool to be followed later that evening with dinner. I also agreed that on the day the rally came to town that she could bring her film crew into the service area and film the event, as long as they did not get in the way. I thought this would be extremely good publicity for Leyland and I later found out that the local dealer was over the moon with the film crew being there as the coverage on the television that night was excellent.

The day the rally was due to arrive I met up with Bill, the Dunlop boys and the Castrol engineers and took them to the yard that I had hired for the day. The owner was there to remove the dogs and we promptly unloaded all the wheels and tyres. There was a new set for each car plus a couple of extras and a few spares as well. If we had no retirements during the day there would be seven cars coming in that evening and I had chosen a couple of the mechanics from the local BL dealership to assist us.

I selected the mechanics after making them race to change a wheel on a car in their workshop. We did not have a Triumph 2.5 available, so I decided to use a Maxi, as one of our entries was a Maxi and it would be good for the mechanics to familiarize themselves with the product that they would have to work on.

So, they all had a go and none of them seemed to have any urgency in the operation whatsoever. The fastest time recorded was 5 min 20 sec. After they had all changed a wheel, I demonstrated how I actually wanted it done and duly changed one myself, only taking 1 min 3 sec. Needless to say, they were all gobsmacked. After witnessing my demonstration, I became like a god to them. They all had so much respect for me that I felt they would have done anything I asked them. One guy offered to introduce me to his sister, but I did not take him up on it.

The boys we had chosen practised and got their times to just under 2 minutes, which was fine and, providing the cars were not delayed, we would have had sufficient time to spend on each car depending on how much time was available to the driver. There was always the possibility that the driver would run out of time, in which case we would have had to do a very quick turn round.

I had also organized a driver to take the drivers to a local hotel in the event that they had sufficient time to take a shower, and we laid on some food and hot and cold drinks as well.

Well, only the girl crew in the Maxi took me up on the showers. They seemed very eager to freshen up and change their clothes and spent just under an hour with me, which gave me time to check the cars over thoroughly.

The service point went well without any complications. We were able to change the front McPherson struts on all the 2.5 Triumphs, check all the brakes and replace a couple of sets of pads, tighten sump guards, clean screens and lights and fill all cars with fuel.

I was thankful that I had had foresight to hire the yard, as there were literally thousands of people about and many of them were pressed up against the fence. There were quite a few there who had recognized me from the television programme the night before and who wanted my autograph.

Once the cars were all through, we packed up and loaded the old wheels and tyres onto the vehicle that Dunlop had hired and handed the yard back to the owner.

I then went down the road to the Ford boys to see if they needed a hand with anything as we always had a very close relationship and knew all the Ford mechanics very well. To my amazement, Anna and her film crew followed me down there, but luckily things had gone well for them so we had a quick beer with them and left.

I went straight back to the hotel arriving about 4 a.m. I had to pack and was due to fly out later that afternoon. Anna was waiting for me and explained that they had got some very unique footage from the service point, which would be shown that night. We had a drink and tumbled into bed for my last fling with her, which turned out to be a very passionate session. In the morning, whilst she was sleeping, I packed and made ready to leave by about 10.30 a.m. so that meant we had a few hours to kill before going to the airport.

There was an overnight stop for the rally in Montevideo and 52 cars had survived, with our cars lying in fourth, seventh, tenth, seventeenth and thirty-sixth. The following morning the rally left Uruguay and headed for Buenos Aires, and some more long stages, but my next port of call was in Bolivia.

Due to the problems we had experienced with immigration on our arrival in Montevideo, we were very concerned that we might have great difficulty in leaving the country. I think someone was looking down on us as everything ran very smoothly and our departure went without a hitch.

My flight from Montevideo to Bolivia was at 4.30 a.m. and I was due to arrive at La Paz airport at around 7.45 a.m. local time. The flight was very smooth and uneventful despite the fact that the plane was in fact very old. I did not know at the time, but the airport is the highest international airport in the world and just under 12,000 feet above sea level.

I always remember the moment that we came in to land at

La Paz. Just as we were about to touch down, one of the passengers, a Bolivian woman, decided she was going to the toilet and got up to everyone's horror. I had to grab her to stop her being thrown down the aisle, which was a bit stupid on my part as I could have easily broken an arm.

Within minutes of the plane touching down, the press, television crews and technicians began to feel sick and nauseous from the lack of oxygen due to the high altitude. We had oxygen pills that we had to take twice a day and it became very obvious that we would have to get used to doing things at a much slower rate here. The locals survived the altitude by chewing the leaves of the marijuana plant and they all looked as though they were on another planet.

Tom and I met up again as Tom had flown in about half an hour before me and had decided to wait for me. We took a taxi together to the hotel, which was located in the centre of the capital. It was a typical tourist hotel, the name of which I cannot remember. There was very little furniture in my room, just a double bed, bedside cabinet and a stand to put my suitcase on. In the en-suite, there was a hand basin, a shower and a toilet. There were, however, a few tiles on the walls, but only where necessary. The construction of the whole hotel appeared to be timber throughout, which was dark and old, but having said all that, it was clean and served its purpose. I just hoped there wouldn't be a fire in the place during our stay.

Tom and I had to take a local flight from La Paz to Potosoi, a tin-mining town. The plane was even older than the previous one, with canvas seats like deck chairs and seatbelts attached to the tubular frame of each seat.

The town was like something out of an old mining town in a movie and we wondered what was in store for us here. It was very difficult to keep your eyes on everything as equipment, spares, tools or anything you had could go missing at any point in time. We were glad we were not staying there as we were due to return to La Paz after the rally had passed through.

The driving skills of all the locals were so bad here that the police decided to cordon off all the roads to give the competitors a quick and safe journey through the town.

This meant that thousands of Bolivians would have to walk, which was actually no different from usual for many of them. The noisy rally cars bellowed through the town, yet the pedestrians all strolled about in the road without a care in the world. Most of them looked high on the cannabis that they seemed to chew all day long. Thousands of small Bolivian women in bowler hats with babies strapped on their backs were coming out of little mud houses all along the route, chattering with curiosity and excitement to see what was going on. This was a spectacle that will remain in my memory for the rest of my life.

For them, it must have been the sight of the century seeing hundreds of young Europeans in multi-coloured racing overalls covered with their sponsors' badges wearing crash helmets in gaudy motor cars, again with their sponsors' names all over. On top of all that, the cars were about 30 years younger than any other vehicle on the roads there.

It was a bitter blow to the team when we received the news that Andrew Cowan had been involved in an accident. Apparently, he had waited for daylight at the start of the stage, as all the crew felt it would be a big advantage as the stage was 510 miles long, a similar distance as Edinburgh to Dover.

Unfortunately, just before the end of the stage he had caught with up an Austin 1800, the Beauty Box, which was the ladies' crew driven by Jean Denton. Blinded by the dust that the 1800 was throwing up, Andrew missed a corner and the car went off the road, landing on its roof, completely wrecking it. All three crew members incurred head injuries and Andrew sustained a cracked vertebra in his neck. They all ended up in hospital where they were very well looked after. Fortunately, they were all released from hospital a few days later.

This information was devastating to the team and a bitter disappointment to me, as I had hoped Andrew would do as well in this marathon as he had done in the last one, which, of course, he had won. However, I was extremely thankful that he had not suffered any major injuries. Later when I saw MY car with the roof and wings all crushed from the accident, I could have cried after all the hours I had spent on it. But that was rallying and the rally had to go on, so in events like this you had to pick yourself up and get on with the job in hand.

At the end of this stage, many of the drivers had to be carried from their cars as they were suffering from exhaustion after 13 hours of competitive driving. Don't forget also that the navigators also had to stay awake to read the pace notes in the high temperatures, which was really telling and exhausting for all the crews.

Tom and I had the same job to carry out again, which was to find a suitable service area and to organize a couple of helpers. There had been a major service point about two hours before they got to us, so we hoped that we would not have to get too involved. There was always the possibility that a vehicle had encountered problems since leaving the last service point. However, we still had to organize the usual thing and be prepared for the inevitable. The crews always took advantage of any food that we made available, and we always had a couple of tyres in case anyone experienced a puncture. Nevertheless, we didn't have enough gear to cover all the eventualities that might arise. This time we were too far from a local hotel to organize showers and a change of clothes.

We found an ideal spot along the road that they came into town on with plenty of space for us to have all the cars in together if need be, although that would have been highly unlikely as they were all spaced out well. But as one or two had retired, the cars had closed up a lot in the past few days. All went very well and we only had a couple of wheels to change and a few adjustments before the cars were on their way again. So, once again, we packed up and made ready to go back to the airport and wait for our next flight.

The next port of call for Tommy and I was Lima in Peru. Fortunately, we had a few days to recuperate from the effects of the high altitude and the traveling, which had made us feel extremely exhausted.

The following day, we took a local flight to Cuzco where the service point was to be set up. This was about 13,000 feet above sea level and, again, it became difficult to keep the energy levels up due to the lack of oxygen.

Cuzco was a very bustling and colourful city with cobbled streets and plenty of busy markets filled with textiles laid out like a huge rainbows. Most of the buildings were very old and the streets looked shabby and dirty. My first impressions of the city were not great and I immediately felt one had to be extremely careful here as nothing looked clean.

There were numerous museums and cafés and it just seemed to be a good place to get acclimatized to the altitude. We spent the first morning sat outside in a café drinking coffee and watching the people, who were dressed in a vast array of colours, all wearing colourful hats. Most of the ladies had babies strapped to their backs.

This time we had no difficulty with the service area as Dunlop had taken over the premises of one of their agents. Tommy and I decided to take the day off and do the tourist thing and visit the City of the Incas at Machu Picchu, 80 km from Cuzco.

We caught the only train, which took us on a spectacular journey as it proceeded on its climb up through the Andes, passing through the Sacred Valley, the bread basket of the Inca civilization, where all sorts of food crops were grown, and stopping at all the stations on route to take on water and coal. The train is known as the Vistadome because each carriage has a glass roof enabling passengers to view the sheer mountain walls along with the many spectacular waterfalls. We eventually arrived at Aguas Calientes, a small ramshackle town just at the base of Macchu Picchu, some four hours later. It was very interesting to see how the Third World population lived in the backwoods of the Andes. At every station the train stopped, the locals came out in force to sell their trinkets, herb tea or cannabis.

It was a very short walk to the ruins from the station and we soon arrived at the city of the Incas. We were greeted by a small fortress sitting majestically between two mountain peaks surrounded by dense vegetation and often shrouded in mist. It was just an amazing scene and so breathtaking that it will remain in my memory forever. It was a magnificent day out and I regret that I did not have a camera with me to capture that magnificent moment.

The train ride home was also very interesting as it only took two hours to return and was a bit hairy at times. But I think it did help us to get used to the thin air much faster.

The service point went without any complications and two of the lads that had joined us had flown up in a chartered five-seated Cessna, which had run into difficulties when landing. Tommy and I were instructed to give our flight tickets to the boss and his colleague, and Tommy and I had to return to Lima in the Cessna.

After we closed the service point, we returned to the hotel

and prepared to return to Lima ready for our onward journey. We had to wait 24 hours for the spare parts to arrive and be fitted to the Cessna before we could take off but, eventually, we were all set to go and we duly took off from Cuzco.

The Cessna spent about half an hour just going round and round in circles so it could get sufficient height to fly over the top of the Andes. This was a bit scary, to say the least. Looking down on all the snowcapped mountains was very eerie, but we eventually gained enough height to continue our journey back to Lima.

Tommy and I then flew from Lima to Columbia, again, in a very old aircraft, again, with the canvas seats. We landed at Cali some two hours later wondering what we would find here. Well, once more, we had rocked up at a city that did not look clean. Poverty seemed to be rife as no one was dressed very well and most people in uniforms looked as though their uniform had been washed draining it of colour, which just made it appear shabby by European standards. The façades of the buildings looked as though they were crumbling and there were signs of masonry on the pavements where it had fallen off. We were warned here not to carry cameras or wear a good wrist watch as getting mugged was a strong possibility.

The service point was organized by the local British Leyland dealer, which saved us having to check out the area and hire staff as anything we wanted was provided. The dealer also made sure that he would benefit from all the publicity he could get from the event.

Once again, the service point went according to plan and we had plenty of time to spend on the cars as they seemed to have spread out a bit from one or two retirements. Apart from the routine checks, wheel changes, checking sump guards, lighting and general tightening, this service point seemed very relaxed compared with some of the others.

Our next port of call was in Nicaragua but we could not fly direct so we had a brief stop off at Panama where we were able to peruse the duty free shops. I have to admit that the prices at the airport were some of the cheapest I have seen and there were some good bargains to be had. I ended up buying a Sony cine camera for about £50.

On arrival in Nicaragua we were met by the local dealer once more and taken to our hotel. One thing that was very noticeable in this country was that there only seemed to be two classes of people again: the very rich and the very poor. This seemed to be the case in many of the South American countries we visited.

The city we travelled to was very clean in comparison to where we were before and the surrounding areas were full of greenery and all kinds of vegetation. There was a real welcoming feeling and I took to it straightaway, although I was very embarrassed with the amount of poor people around. Being a European, the poor people considered us to be rich, and we probably were comparing our standards with theirs and consequently were bothered a bit by beggars, especially those close to the hotel.

We stayed at the Intercontinental Hotel, which had been

built in the shape of a pyramid. It was a spectacular building and the height of luxury, which we both enjoyed to the full.

At the weekend, the dealer took Tommy and I to his private lake, which was probably the size of Lake Coniston, where he had two very big power boats that he used for water-skiing and high-speed performance, housed in a huge boathouse. His wife and two daughters joined us later, bringing with them the most magnificent picnic. It included lobster, smoked salmon, crab, suckling pig, beef, pork, freshly baked bread and all the exotic fruit that one could dream off. There was also champagne and beer by the bucketful to wash it all down. Needless to say, we had a marvellous day and we were totally relaxed and ready for the next service point.

At this stage of the rally, the cars were beginning to suffer and looked very tired, which was not surprising with the terrain encountered, but we kept putting them back together and they kept running.

Once again most of the work covered was routine apart from changing the Macpherson struts on the Triumphs, which were taking a bit of a bashing. We had changed these frequently so we had had plenty of practise and we had got the replacement time down to about 15 minutes, which I thought was good going, although it was never fast enough for the drivers or navigators.

As soon as the service point closed, Tommy and I packed everything away and made our way back to the hotel, relaxed in the bar, enjoyed a good meal and packed our cases for our departure the following day to our last point of call, Mexico, where again we separated and covered two different locations.

On arrival in Mexico City airport, we made our way to the Camino Real Hotel, another luxurious place to stay. The whole team assembled there for the last service point or to relax before the return journey.

The city itself was a magnificent display of stunning architecture. It was all very old but a lot cleaner than what we had been used to in the poorer countries of South America. The locals were friendlier and looked much happier, probably due to the fact that there seemed to be more work there in comparison, and people had more money. I loved Mexico City; there just seemed to be a very welcoming aura about it.

My last service point was about 200 miles from Mexico City and I had to meet up with Jeremy Ferguson, the Competition manager of Dunlop Tyre Company, first. Jeremy had hired a Ford Mustang from the local hire company at the hotel and as soon as we were given the keys, we duly set off for what we thought was to be an uneventful trip.

All went well at the service point and was purely routine. It was just a question of making sure that the cars completed the last leg of the journey without any incident and to ensure that they got to Mexico safely and on time.

We left the service point at about 1 a.m. to drive back to the hotel and get a few hours' sleep if that was possible. We had been motoring for about half an hour and I was drifting in and out of sleep, which was not unusual for me, when I heard Jeremy shout followed by a tremendous thud. I just caught sight of a horse going over the top of us. Apparently Jeremy had taken the corner a bit too fast and there in the middle of the road was this Mustang, which he could not avoid. Consequently we hit it head on, so to speak. The Mustang went over the bonnet, screen and roof, and, whilst there was an awful lot of blood about and despite searching the verges in the dark, we weren't able to find the Mustang afterwards.

However, the car was a complete mess and not drivable at all as the fan had been pushed back into the radiator, the screen had shattered from the distortion of the body shell and the roof panel, and, from my experience, the car would have been considered a write-off. There still remained 150 miles to travel back to Mexico City and we could not have chosen a more remote area to be in if we had tried. The moon and stars were shining bright and there was not a street light, house or building to be seen anywhere on the horizon.

One or two drivers stopped to see if we were alright but none offered us a lift back to the city. Then, to our surprise and delight, a Greyhound bus suddenly appeared around the bend and we waved it down. Fortunately, the driver stopped and was very sympathetic to our tale. He informed us that it was not uncommon on that stretch of road for that type of accident to occur. He agreed to take us to the city and allow us to pay our fare at the ticket office on arrival, so luckily we were able to continue on our journey. We managed a little sleep on the coach and arrived in Mexico City at about 6 a.m. We paid our dues and took a taxi to the hotel where we checked in and caught up on our sleep.

Apparently, Jeremy informed the hire company at the hotel of the location of their car and explained to them what had happened and left them to sort it out.

The rally finished at the Aztec Stadium. Only 23 cars actually made it to the finish line out of the 92 starters, with ours ending up second, fourth, tenth and 22nd. We also picked up two class wins to complete the picture.

Two days after the finish, the team was invited to a party at the residence of the British Military Attaché. We all decided to attend, although it was not really our scene. However, we acted like good ambassadors; well-mannered, polite and chatted to all the other guests whilst sipping our cocktails, all the while dying to swap the posh drinks for a good pint of beer.

On the Saturday, we all checked out of the hotel and made our way to the airport in a coach that had been hired for the journey. Once at the airport we learnt that the Britannia, having travelled to Montreal with a cargo of cigarettes, had unfortunately flown into a flock of birds on landing, which had resulted in a broken windscreen.

In order not to delay the return to the UK and to speed things up, we were flown to Montreal on a Braniff

International DC8. After a short delay in Canada, we eventually boarded the Britannia for the 14-hour flight to London, Gatwick. Because of the delay, Caledonian Airways gave us a free bar for the entire journey home. To break the boredom of the flight, we kept the hostess busy serving drinks whilst the team went through their repertoire of songs. I do not think any one of us managed to get any sleep on this return flight.

At Gatwick, we were met by a coach that took us to London to a reception hosted by Lord Stokes at the Lancaster Hotel. Later that afternoon, the coach took us all back to Abingdon, with most of us three parts to the wind as we had all been drinking for the past 18 hours. We were eventually dropped off at our homes, which was a welcome site as most of us had been away for over 13 weeks.

Looking through the log that I kept of all my flights, I was shocked to see that I had been on 34 separate flights with 18 different airlines.

Marathon de la Route - Nurburgring

Two cars were entered for this event. The first was a Mini Clubman 1275 to be driven by John Hanley, Alec Poole and Julien Verneave. The second car was a Rover V8 4.3 litre, prepared by Bill Shaw. This second car was then transported to Abingdon for Lucas to finish off the wiring, and I was also in charge of finishing off with a few jobs here and there. This gave us the opportunity to familiarize ourselves with the product before the race.

The reason why Bill Shaw was mentioned and not the Competitions Department is because Bill had a very good reputation within the racing fraternity for preparing a very good race car. Bill produced the car with a 4.3 Rover/Buick engine, but, while it was being prepared, Peter Browning sent a couple of engines to Traco Engineering in the USA. On their return, however, it was found that they didn't produce as much power as the one prepared by Bill anyway.

We took the car to the Goodwood Race Circuit where Roy Pierpoint, who was to drive the car at Nurburgring, put the car through its paces. The only problem that Roy reported was a propshaft vibration, so we ordered a new one from Hardy Spicer that was specially balanced just for the job. We hoped that the new shaft would arrive before the team set off for Germany.

I did not attend this event as I had booked a two-week holiday in Dawlish Warren with the family, a favourite haunt of mine that we had visited for the last couple of years.

At Nurburgring, the scrutinizing went exceptionally well but the new prop shaft had not arrived from the manufacturer. When it did, Den Green immediately flew to Liege, was met at the airport and taken to a pre-determined spot in the forest close to the where a service crew were waiting to replace it. The race cars left Liege on a gentle drive to the circuit, and although there was no permitted service point on route, the team guided the Rover into the forest where they set to and changed the prop shaft.

The 86-hour race started at 1 a.m. The Rover and the Mini

were positioned on the second row of the grid behind a team of Porsches. The circuit was 17.68 miles per lap and the cars roared off into the night. We expected the Rover to be lapping around 13.5 to 14 minutes per lap. Well, everyone was so surprised that on the first lap the Rover led way out in front. The team thought that there had been a multiple accident holding the rest of the pack up.

Seconds later, the Mini arrived with the rest of the cars on its heels. This was great for the team, who had been demoralized by the recent announcement received whilst on the ferry that the department would soon close.

At the driver changeover, the fast lapping times were discussed and Roy pointed out that whilst lapping at around 13 minutes, the car was cruising. The Mini was also going well, but the team was not so confident of the staying power of the car and they felt that it would suffer later on in the race.

At 9 a.m. the Mini came into the pits with severe overheating. It was quickly diagnosed that the head gasket had failed and the team attempted to change it in the 15 minutes permissible. It took 25 minutes, so the car was out of time, but they sent it out for one last lap to prove that it was still running before it retired.

The Rover, however, was still powering through the field, but the special prop shaft had not cured the problem and the team kept a close watch on the prop and the tail end of the gearbox casing for fear of it breaking up. After sixteen hours, the car had a lead of three laps, but regrettably the vibration was getting worse and it was decided to retire before the gearbox shattered and covered the track with oil. This was a tremendous performance and all concerned thought that the car had a good future in the endurance races. Unfortunately, with the closure of the department, this was unlikely to happen.

The Closure

When we returned home from holiday, there was a pile of post on the mat (as always). Among the letters was one from the M.G. Car Company. Its contents shocked me: the department was to be closed at the end of October and I was to be made redundant, unless a suitable job could be found for me within the factory.

You can imagine how I felt on returning to work the following Monday, when it was confirmed that the company would do all in its power to find me suitable alternative employment. All personnel affected (and those that did not want the jobs offered to them) were given redundancy packages at the government's recommended levels: there would be no enhancements. We all knew that there was little likelihood of the company finding suitable jobs for skilled men within the factory: we were stuck between a rock and a hard place.

Approximately one month before the closure of the department, Peter Browning resigned as Competition manager because the company refused to approve a long-term programme. Such a plan, Peter felt, was necessary to restore the morale in the workshop, and instil some confidence in the future.

The company offered me a job as progress chaser, ferrying cars from the production line to a waiting compound no more than a two-minute drive away. My pig-headedness got the better of me. I thought that both the company and the trade union had behaved disgracefully. Some of the affected people were highly skilled; the company had spent millions training its staff, including me, and now it was effectively closing us down. Consequently, I did not hesitate to tell the company exactly what I thought of the situation, and what they could do with the job on offer. I opted for redundancy, and received a grand total of £312 for my 15 years of service.

On reflection, I should have taken the job offered while looking for a better opportunity either within the factory or outside. And, I soon discovered that the hours and wages were much better in the factory than elsewhere.

Life in the Retail Trade

When I left Competitions I did not find it too difficult to find another job. Several dealers had been in touch with the department, offering jobs to those that were prepared to move out of the vicinity. I had an interview with Marshalls of Cambridge, but I did not fancy moving my family to that area. Instead, I accepted an offer from Cherwell Motors. This was a Routes dealership on the Banbury Road, Oxford, and suited me better: I didn't want to commute too far, and needed time to decide my future. Two other mechanics, Derrick Plummer and Mick Hogan, also took jobs at the dealership.

Though some unfamiliar vehicles to me – such as the

Hillman Imp – proved difficult to work on, in general the work was relatively easy. The work didn't really suit me, though, and I quickly came to hate my job. For ten years, I had worked in the very clean environment of the Competitions Department. In the retail workshop things were very different, and I hated getting so dirty every day.

The foreman there was very good and appreciated that we were all much quicker working on the Leyland vehicles. Every job was allocated a time by which it was expected to be completed. The times that were set by the manufacturer were fairly tight, and fast work earned a bonus. Speaking with other mechanics in the workshop, the only way to make the bonus was to take short-cuts – a practice totally alien to the three of us.

Sadly, the sudden change placed an enormous strain on my marriage to Jean. We were both finding my being at home every day difficult to adjust to, and tensions between us quickly rose.

On 4 December 1971, I was blessed with the arrival of my second son Matthew; but home life was extremely difficult. I was now earning about a third of what I had been used to, and having to make some severe cut-backs in spending that served only to add to the stress.

I continued my search for another job and had several interviews. Finally, I decided to accept a position as a reception engineer at Eyles and Coxeter, London Road, Headington, Oxford, which was part of Chiltern Motor Holdings, the local Triumph dealership. At the time, the group had five dealerships, two of which were in Oxford, two in Reading, and one in Bicester.

This job proved to be much better. The larger group seemed more organized and certainly took customer service to another level. However, even though the pay was better than on the shop floor in the garage, it was still a lot less than I had been used to in the Competitions Department.

Later that year, Derrick and I started our own company, D.P. Tuning (named so because of our initials). Some of our old colleagues had recommended us to Jean Denton, one of the private owners. She asked for an estimate to prepare her MG Midget for the Tulip Rally. Once the estimate had been agreed, the car was delivered to Derrick's house. We set about the task of rebuilding Jean Denton's car in Derrick's enormous garage and employed Mick Hogan to help us. The job only took a couple of months.

During those two months spent working on the Midget, word of mouth increased our client base. Needing new, larger premises to enable our rapid expansion, we eventually took an offer extended by Sandy Lawson, once the secretary to the competitions manager, to house our operation in one of her garages at Chandlers Farm in Bagley Wood, near Oxford.

The location, approximately midway between our homes, was ideal, and within a week we had moved in and set up our workshop. Immediately I began earning a second wage, which made up the shortfall between what I was earning and what I had been used to previously.

There was always a problem when picking up vehicles, but that was something that we got used to. Often the car belonged to a friend of a friend, so making flexible arrangements was never difficult.

The job at Eyle & Coxeter was going well, too, and after about three months I was asked to transfer to the city branch in Park End Street outside the city centre. This dealership had Jaguar, Rover, and Triumph franchises and I was appointed as senior reception engineer. One of the engineers at the branch, Dave, who was already working in reception, was a bit hurt that he had not been considered for the job, and this caused some friction between us. In the end though, everything worked out well and we became good friends.

Park End Street was an extremely busy workshop. The location was on the main trunk road through Oxford, so there was no parking on the roads adjacent to the dealership; and the traffic wardens made certain that you didn't. They would often spend most of their day walking up and down outside. In fairness, they always came in and told us to move a car before issuing a ticket. The parking problem was soon to be resolved; a year after starting at Park End Street, we learned that we would be relocated to new premises at Pear Tree Roundabout on Oxford's ringroad inside a further six months.

Now separated from Jean, I was living at Marston where I rented a room with friends in Ferry Road. Moving out of the family home was the most difficult decision I have ever made and it really upset me leaving the two boys, particularly as my youngest son, Matthew, was only a few weeks old; but I could see the ill-effects that our constant arguments were having on my eldest son Andrew.

Unfortunately, my wife concluded that as I had moved out of the matrimonial home I had given up all my rights to see the children. I was devastated by her decision – my boys meant everything to me. I decided very quickly that under no circumstances was I going to lose them.

I had a long chat with my solicitor and we went through all the procedures for legal aid in Reading, which I was eventually granted. We were able to take Jean to the county court so that I could have the access I was entitled to as their father. This was a very confusing time in my life, as there was so much happening at the same time, both professionally and personally.

On the day of the hearing, I was extremely nervous as we found out that the judge sitting that day had a reputation for ruthlessness. As it happened, this worked in my favor, as the first question the judge asked was who was representing both parties. My barrister stood up and introduced himself as acting on my behalf, stating that the other party did not appear to be in the courtroom.

My barrister had discussed this scenario with me prior to the hearing, and we expected the hearing to be postponed. Instead of this postponement, the judge stated that he had read the files on the case and found it extremely frustrating that the other party, defending, could not be bothered to turn up in court. After a pause, he passed a verdict that, under the circumstances and as my request for access was very reasonable, he would grant the custody order we had presented with immediate effect.

Whilst it was a very expensive day in court (£3,000, which in 1972 was a lot of money), I felt it was the best three grand I had ever spent. I spent the next two years paying it back to the legal aid department, but today I have the benefit of enjoying two loving sons and their lovely families.

D.P. Tuning was also flourishing, and our clientele had grown beyond all expectations; we were approaching a scenario where we were going to be able to choose which jobs we wanted.

While I was considering which way I wanted my career to develop, I was summoned to our head office in Reading and the group MD offered me the service manager's position at the new premises, which was to be the flagship of the group.

There was, of course, a down side to all this: the group's head office was also going to be located on the same site as the directors, meaning I'd be under scrutiny all day and every day.

This helped me arrive at my decision about D.P. Tuning, and Derek and I decided to close the business. We ran it down over the following few weeks and went our separate ways, though I am thankful to say that Derek's family are still good friends to this day. Unfortunately, Derek suddenly passed away whilst I was writing this book.

The new premises opened and the directors had decided to hold a wine and cheese evening to mark the occasion. We had quite a night with many of our regular clients, fleet clients, and numerous members of senior management from Jaguar, Rover and Triumph.

After the opening night, I had a mammoth job on hand to make this huge workshop pay for itself and, more to the point, make a profit. It was at this time that I realized I had had no management skills or any management training whatsoever. So I contacted the group training manager and discussed the problem with him. Fortunately, he agreed to let me manage my own training schedule. He gave me an open cheque book to attend the management courses I wanted, and I was allowed to utilize the British Leyland Training College at Haisley Manor just outside of Warwick.

I decided to start with a Service Manager's course to see where this took me. I asked the course tutor which courses he could recommend that would be beneficial to me for the future. This resulted in me doing a follow-up course for Advanced Service Management, along with Budgeting, Profit Planning, Service Management Accounts, and Service Marketing. It seemed I was always at Haisley Manor undertaking training. The staff there knew me by my Christian name and would always make some comment when I arrived for another course.

I have to admit that the two most useful courses were the Budgeting and Profit Planning, and Management Accounts.

The budgeting course gave me some formulae that made

the annual event of preparing budgets for the department for the following year very easy. These were usually undertaken in October/November, and my MD could never understand how I could do them so quickly nor, if he rejected them, how I could do a revised version almost by return. I did learn that whilst I could do them quickly, a lot of the service managers in the group struggled with them. I learned to hang on to them for a few days before submitting.

As for the Management Accounts course, this was probably the most beneficial. I could now fully understand the accounts that the management accountant put before me each month. I was paid a bonus of 10% of the amount by which I beat my budget, which would be scrutinized monthly. With my new knowledge, I had the ability and confidence to query or refuse to accept things being dumped in my department's accounts. This used to create one or two arguments, but at the end of the day I always won.

I was very fortunate that I had a very good team working for me: the foreman was extremely competent; my reception engineers, led by Dave Williams, who was exceptionally good with people; Terry Field, my warranty clerk, was also extremely good in this major role of any service department – you could lose pounds on payments from the factory if you did not keep on top of it, and, fortunately, Terry was one step ahead of us all. My secretary, Linda, made the job very easy for me with her efficiency – presenting me with my diary first thing each morning, or client reminder letters to sign, she was always on the ball, and I believe that we had the perfect working relationship. If she ever heard of any issues through the grapevine, she would be sure to inform me so that I could prepare for the problem. All the above were a fabulous team, extremely loyal, and made my job easy for me.

There were only two clients that Dave would not get involved with. Firstly, an eccentric woman who ran an old E-Type Jaguar: she was completely scatty. Her E-Type was not the most reliable and was always letting her down. She always wanted our services, yet she never had any money and wanted us to do everything on the cheap. When Dave saw her coming, he would always call for me. On one occasion in mid-summer, she came bouncing into the showroom in my direction, wearing a bright red plastic mackintosh and a sou'wester hat. I had to think quickly – this was either going to be very embarrassing or I could turn it in my favour. I decided to greet her in the middle of the showroom and proceeded to kiss her on both cheeks. This change in behaviour towards her meant, from that day on, she never gave me a single problem and always seemed relaxed in our company.

The other was an estate agent with a Jaguar XJ6 who was extremely arrogant and always had a fat cigar in his mouth blowing ash everywhere when he spoke to you. The car was new, but the interior was a far cry from its original state, with cigar ash everywhere, the ashtray full of old cigars, and a general stale and disgusting smell. Luckily for Dave, this client would usually go straight to Linda and ask her if I was in the office; and she would come and find me so that I could look after him. I would do so, of course, but I have to admit that he was the most arrogant man that I had come across in my life.

After a couple of years, Dave decided to resign in a bid to fulfil his ambition of a cycle trip around Europe with his brother. Dave was greatly missed as he was exceptionally good at his job.

Although I was the service manager for this branch, I somehow managed to also take responsibility in all matters involving the site, which included a huge forecourt and petrol station. Such matters varied from problems with the vending machines to new cars being broken into in the compound, or water leaks in the roof of the building.

After a couple of years as service manager of the Roundabout, I was given an additional service department to look after at Cherwell Drive. This site had five fuel pumps, two service bays and a tyre-fitting bay. The service bay seemed to be performing well with more hours being sold than were available. However I was not happy with the tyre sales, which, in a nutshell, were pathetic. To be fair no one took much notice of the place unless it made a loss and the director involved would want to off-load it on to someone else. We were lucky at the start if we sold 20 tyres a month – I wanted this figure trebled in as many months and by the end of the twelve months trading, I aimed to be selling a figure of around 150 a month.

Therefore, the first instruction I gave to my service department at the Roundabout was that all tyres must be purchased through Cherwell Drive. This was a logical step and I knew it would inevitably increase sales dramatically. The director agreed that this was a good move and that all the service departments in Oxford would follow suit. I also stated that in order to increase sales, it was essential that we were competitive with the other local tyre suppliers.

I also figured that the quantities of tyres that we were buying from our supplier were low, and as a result we were not being offered the best price for the product. This made it impossible for us to be competitive with other suppliers in the area.

At the time, the company had a very strong relationship with Total Oil and they were buying tyres direct from Michelin. They were offering them to establishments like ours at a very competitive price. Another benefit was that they actually invoiced you three months later, which in effect gave you three months credit. So the plan was to sell the stock we had bought before we paid for them.

I felt that this was a good system and looked at the history of what we had been selling and immediately purchased two months; worth of stock. As we were purchasing greater quantities, the effect of this put us into a different discount bracket. For the first time, the department had tyres in stock and did not have to order them in especially for the client, which meant they were 30% cheaper. Very quickly the tyre sales went up to sixty a month. But I then ran into a storage problem. The department did not have room to store more than seventy tyres, but due to the stock turnover, we set up an arrangement with Total on the delivery. Their workers were now very stretched with their work load, but had seen a rapid increase in their bonus payments and therefore did not object. They didn't have the capacity for any more stock unless they employed additional personnel, which wasn't an option as the figures from the service bay were less efficient although remained very profitable. The situation left the department with merely skeletal staff, and when an employee took holiday leave, I'd have to temporarily transfer a member of staff from the Roundabout.

Four months into having responsibility of Cherwell, I had a call from a contact at Thames Valley Police Force informing me that there was a tender out to supply a batch of tyres. I immediately made contact and asked if I could quote for the supply of these tyres. He agreed that it would be in order and gave me a list of their requirements of various sizes that totalled 3,000 tyres. He also advised that I would have to be extremely competitive as many of the major suppliers in Oxford were also quoting.

Well, I had some fun with this and wrote into my quote all the bonuses that I would get from Total, who also had a sliding scale that gave me a greater discount the more that I purchased. As luck would have it, that particular month Total was giving an extra bonus on batches of twenty tyres purchased. I decided that if I won the tender, I would purchase three month's stock, giving me a better price than any other order could offer. The buying price enabled me to quote for each tyre size at the agreed price with Total, which included an extra £1.00 discount per tyre purchased that month. On this quantity, I was set to make a minimum of £3,000 on the supply of the tyres to the police, plus all the benefits and bonuses on whatever tyres I ordered for stock.

To cut the story short, I won the quote – much to the surprise of the other suppliers, who could not believe I had managed to undercut them. I ordered the tyres and three days later a lorry arrived on the forecourt with the goods. I made a quick decision to call the police workshop and arranged for the lorry driver, having given him a gratuity, to follow me to the police HQ about two miles away. The tyres were duly unloaded and I returned to the Roundabout having cleared £3,000 profit without so much as touching the tyres, and also gained 120 tyres for stock at prices I would never match again.

Fortunately, Thames Valley Police paid for the goods before we received the bill from Total Oil. On the strength of this sale, I won a thoroughly enjoyable long weekend in Jersey at the expense of Total Oil. I have to admit that I always enjoyed wheeling and dealing in any aspect of the job.

I met my second wife, and after 4 years of living together we decided to get married. We were married at the Bicester registry office and then went to the Mitre Hotel in Oxford, a Berni Inn, accompanied with 20 of our close friends and family. You may well ask, why a Berni Inn? Well, it was quite simple really. The manager there was a client of mine and I used to look after his Mini for him, never charging for what I had done, and in return he would not charge me when I went to the Berni Inn. On this occasion however, I did pay a large contribution towards the meal.

My wife and I bought a spacious, semi-detached house with three bedrooms at Kidlington in a quiet cul-de-sac. The house had a large-sized garden and some superb neighbours.

My wife worked in the insurance industry in Oxford and had a very good job; but after a couple of years the office closed and she joined a broker on the Banbury Road, Oxford, where she later became a director.

The Chiltern Group had gone through a franchise problem as British Leyland had decided to reorganize the franchises in Oxford and awarded the Jaguar, Rover and Triumph franchise to the Hartwell Motor Group. Both Hartwell Group and Oxford Distributor had been trying to get the Jaguar, Rover and Triumph franchise for years. Hartwell's then purchased the dealership that Chiltern Motor Holding had on the Botley Road, which was a prime site in Oxford. Chiltern Motor Holdings then moved the General Motor dealership to the Roundabout and purchased another dealership on the Iffley Road that belonged to the Hartwell Group. At the same time, they purchased Morris Garages at Newbury, keeping the Rover Triumph franchise.

When the company took over the Newbury branch, the warranty claims were in a poor state with over £21,000 outstanding. I was approached by the group managing director, who asked for my knowledge in this field and assistance in resolving the situation.

After inspecting the documentation, I identified that the problem was much bigger than expected. A vast amount of the claims had passed their submission date and so my immediate thoughts were that I was going to need a lot of help. So I made contact with a colleague I dealt with in Rover Triumph customer service, who looked after warranty matters for the dealer network and had also become a good friend over the years. I explained the situation to him and asked for his advice, and whether there was anything he could do to help me.

In return for helping me resolve the situation, I offered to pick up the full cost for a couple of nights out in Redditch, covering everything from a decent meal, nightclub, and the hotel bill for two rooms. I approached my MD and reassured him that the outstanding warranty claims would be resolved within a couple of weeks, but in the meantime he was to accept all my expenses that month without question. Of course, he initially queried my intentions, but I assured him that all would be above board and he was not to worry. He reluctantly agreed and the plans were made.

The Friday in question came and I set off to Redditch to the hotel to meet my pal and his girlfriend. We spent a little while going through the claims over a drink in the bar. After passing 90% of them he advised that he would have to take the others into the office on Monday to look at them, and that he may have to reject a few in order for all to appear genuine. We then had dinner and headed round the corner to the nightclub, where we stayed until the early hours of the morning before returning to the hotel.

After a hearty breakfast we parted company and went our separate ways. I was feeling content and successful — I'd set out what I wanted to do and achieved my goal, and I knew my boss would be delighted with the result.

On the Monday morning I presented my MD with the claims that had been passed and told him that I had spent just under £300 in getting the claims authorized and that the remaining 10% of claims were being analysed that same day. The only comment he made was, "I do not know how you sleep at night." To this, I could only respond that I would sleep better if I were not given other people's mistakes to correct. In total, the final amount of claims passed was £19,650, which I felt was more than acceptable under the circumstances.

After five years in the job and approaching 37, I decided that I ought to look at my future, taking into consideration that I may not have many more opportunities for a career change.

At the time, the group was changing dramatically with new directors being brought in who were more profit-orientated and did not have the same attitude towards customer service as their predecessors. I personally did not like this new attitude, and, what with directors' offspring completing their university degrees and gaining direct access into the business, I could not see my career progressing further than service manager within the group.

I recall an incident involving the group MD's daughter, whom the GMD had requested I find some work for during her university vacations. I invited the young lady in for an interview to see where her capabilities would fit in with the business. After a chat with her I decided that it would be a good opportunity to update my customer filing system, and as she was going to be working in public view of the reception area it was necessary for her to dress accordingly, and asked her to respect this. However, about ten days into her placement, she arrived one morning in jeans. Linda, my secretary, came in to my office and warned that I had a problem on my hands – the other girls in the area did not take too kindly to Kate wearing jeans and rebelliously stated that they too would wear jeans the following day.

I asked Linda to send Kate in to see me and pointed out to her that whilst she looked very good in jeans, I did not like them in the public area and asked that she go home and change. She told me that she had come in with her father and had no way of getting home, so I promptly called for the company chauffeur to take her home to change. After lunch, the group managing director came into my office and said that he understood I had a problem with Kate that morning, to which I replied, "No, not really; it was just that I did not like her wearing jeans in the reception area." He just shrugged his shoulders and left my office. Most people within the company thought that this was not a good career move, but I was adamant that she would conform to the rules as did the rest of the staff.

There was another occasion when we were in a group service managers meeting and a new director wanted to inform us all of his future plans. He had planned to implement certain changes and so long as he received no negative feedback or objections he would implement them forthwith. He was a very arrogant person who tended to bully people, and most of the managers were very apprehensive and afraid of him. During the meeting, he started to go through his list of proposed changes, to which nobody spoke up. Then he got to a subject that was dear to my heart: the recovery system operated by each branch. His proposal was to do away with all the recovery vehicles that the company had and sublet all recoveries to an outside source. He finished his speech and immediately concluded, "OK, if we have no objections, the motion is passed."

With that, I saw red and asked him to slow down, stating that I felt he was not letting us participate in the meeting. I also pointed out to him that as part of our contract with the manufacturers we were to provide a recovery service to our clients on their behalf. After taking my opinion and advice on board, the director confirmed that the recovery business would stay at the Roundabout under my supervision and the subject was closed.

I also said to the other meeting attendees in the room, with the director present, that they had to speak up with their opinions as it was vital that we all put our point of view across, enabling the director to accurately analyse the feedback; if we didn't, then we would have to accept his decisions and their consequences.

For me, that meeting made my mind up and each week I would scan the Motoring News (a weekly magazine produced for the motor industry which always had a lot of situations vacant advertised). Week after week there was nothing that took my fancy. Then one week I saw the advert for a works manager at Citroën UK based in Slough,

Buckinghamshire.

Whilst I admit I did not know anything about the Citroën products and was not very enamoured with the cars, I felt the job was a tremendous challenge. So I decided to apply, sent off my CV and waited. At the end of August 1980, I received a telephone call from the personnel director's secretary at Citroën inviting me to attend an interview the following week.

When I attended, I endured a gruelling few hours with the personnel director and I in turn put numerous questions to him, which I had prepared beforehand. I was amazed that he could not answer many of the questions I had prepared on Health and Safety. He called the aftersales director and asked him to come to his office and it appeared that the PD was palming me off on him. The ASD took me round the premises and showed me the areas that I would be responsible for. I felt that the interview, which lasted three hours, had gone exceptionally well and I then returned to Oxford to await the result.

Having had my first interview in September I received a letter a week later to be told that the head office of Citroën in Paris had put an embargo on employing any additional staff. However, they advised that they wanted to put my name on file for a future date when the embargo would be lifted. This was a bitter disappointment as I did not know if I was being fobbed off or whether it was genuine. So I started to scan the papers again for situations vacant.

My suspicions were lifted in December, when I had a

telephone call from the Citroën personnel department inviting me to another interview, since the embargo had been lifted on the position of works manager in particular. That following week I attended the second interview and this time it was only with the aftersales director. After four hours of discussions we knew everything we wanted to know about each other and I felt confident that the interview had gone well enough to expect a job offer within a few days.

As I had predicted, three days later I had a letter offering me the job along with the terms and the conditions. On top of that, the salary was more than twice the money I was currently earning with the Chiltern Group, which on its own was worth thinking about. The offer also requested I commence my employment on the 3 March.

In that same week, I received a letter from the Jury Selection Office instructing me to attend jury service on 27 February at 10.00 a.m. at Oxford Crown Court. This instruction pointed out that it was possible for me to be at their service for the complete period of the hearing that I was assigned to. I promptly wrote to the jury service and explained my situation, which my MD at the time confirmed. Lo and behold, a few days later I received a letter excusing me from the jury service on the dates they had given me. To this day I have never been called upon again to perform this service.

I then prepared my letter of resignation, wording it very carefully, and handed it to my MD. He was very disappointed and said that he would inform the other directors of my decision. It was approximately one hour later that I was summoned to the group MD's office, where the MD also stated his disappointment and asked me to withdraw my letter of resignation. I explained to him that I did not agree with how the group was changing under the jurisdiction of the new directors' attitudes.

Within hours, I had directors approaching me, questioning why I did not like the way they worked, and who was I to judge them. I simply responded that they had just answered their own question.

Citroën UK Ltd.

On 3 March 1981, I joined Citroën UK Ltd. as the workshop manager. On that first morning as an employee of the company, Citroën had arranged for one of the aftersales managers that lived in Oxford to pick me up and take me to Slough, so that I did not have to worry about transport. This was very considerate of the company and of course very useful as I used the journey to my advantage to learn a lot from this guy about Citroën and its personnel, and he in turn was anxious to find out all he could about me.

On arrival, I completed numerous forms for the personnel department and then went straight to the office of the aftersales director, Emile Dubois. He informed me of his plans to send me to Amsterdam for three months' training with Citroën Amsterdam. He felt that being trained by others would be of more benefit to me as opposed to being trained by my own staff, which I had to agree made sense. He also clarified that I would be permitted to fly home every other weekend, returning to Amsterdam on the Monday. He asked if I had any problems with these arrangements and whether my wife would have any objections. Obviously, it did not go down too well at home as it was unexpected; but as I had just started a new job, I could hardly say no to him and we accepted the challenge.

I then met all the directors over lunch in their restaurant. In the afternoon, Emile took me to all the departments within the company, taking the rest of the day to introduce me to every employee that worked there. There were approximately 120 people working at head office and 60 of them would be working directly under me. He also took me to the fleet administrator who gave me a Citroën 2CV to use for the week until I went to Holland.

A week later I was in Amsterdam, and it was not long before I had a string of friends there. I spent hardly any of my free time in the evenings and weekends alone, as there were many invitations to social events with my new acquaintances.

The itinerary involved spending a few weeks in each department, gaining technical training and hands-on experience for each section. Whenever an interesting job came along, I would be moved to that department so that I could gain experience in the job in question. For example, the opportunity arose for me to be involved in changing a longeron, which runs the full length of the chassis of a Citroën CX Prestige. This procedure was not uncommon as they were part of the safety crumple zone and always collapsed in the event of the car being involved in a front-end accident. This involved separating the body shell from the chassis, which was quite a time-consuming job and kept me occupied for several days.

I also got involved with the running problems with gas conversions, which Citroën were heavily occupied with. The company actually had a production line for the GSA and the CX models in the workshop for these conversions to be undertaken. At the time, the Dutch were into gas-converted cars in a big way as the percentage of emissions were a lot lower than other fuels around at the time and the gas was considerably cheaper.

On another occasion, I was involved in the rebuild of a BX that had been involved in a side impact and I saw it through to the completion, including the paintwork. The accident repair manager for Citroën Amsterdam became a close friend of mine and we spent quite a lot free time together. He invited me to spend the weekend with his family just outside of Amsterdam, and when I arrived at his house on the Friday evening I was introduced to his twin daughters who were 20 years of age. Although they weren't identical, they were both very attractive, petite, about 5'5" and weighing around 55 kilos, with long hair to their shoulders and wearing the same dress. They were both developing into lovely young ladies.

His wife was also very petite and I guessed she was around 44 years old. She was taller than her daughters, had short hair and was very well dressed, in a youthful way similar to her daughters. Her dress finished just above the knees, but she had nice legs so it complimented her. All of the ladies had nice figures, which they displayed in their tight-fitting clothes, although this was not unusual for the Dutch ladies.

That evening over dinner with all the family, he explained to me that they were all attending a wedding the following day and that the invitation had also been extended to me, which I duly accepted. During dinner, a lot of sexual connotations were being exchanged and the conversation progressed onto different races. They were discussing the differences in performance in bed, including stamina – or lack of it. It was interesting to note that they did not rate the British men, stating that in their estimation they were not good lovers. I was actually thinking at the time where, or how, this conversation was going to end. The Dutch are a very liberated race and I did not read too much into the conversation, but it did make for a fun and enjoyable evening.

However, in the early hours of the morning, I was woken by the opening of my bedroom door. Peering into the darkness I could see the silhouette of one of the girls in the open doorway entering my room. I could see that she was wearing very little clothing.

I lay very still and pretended to be asleep, waiting to see what she was going to do. I felt the covers being pulled back and she got into bed with me; it was not long before I felt her hands exploring my body. Before long, I could not contain myself any longer – I just had to give in to her.

Suddenly, I realized that there were more than two hands exploring my body. I realised that while I was playing asleep I had not seen the other twin enter the room. She too had got into bed with us. I thought for one brief moment that all my birthdays and Christmases had come at once.

It was the first time that I had ever been involved in a threesome with two girls and it soon became apparent that they had much more stamina than I had, but I am pleased to say that I did not let myself, or my country, down. I will not go into the details of this sexual encounter, but it was one that I have never forgotten, and I am sure that all you readers have a good and vivid imagination. It is one of the few encounters where I have experienced a girl riding me whilst the other was also being extremely demanding.

We were woken at about 8 o'clock by the mother bringing me a cup of tea. When she spotted the girls, she harshly instructed something I could not understand. The girls quickly got out of bed and left the room – but what happened next completely took me by surprise. The mother put the tea on the bedside cabinet, then began to take off her dressing gown, revealing her naked body underneath, before joining me in bed. I decided that it must be the Dutch air that made all the ladies so active and wished I could take some back with me to the UK (the air, that is – not the ladies).

It was a good job that I had managed to get a couple of hours' sleep as the mother was as energetic as her twins and I had to repeat the whole performance again. We eventually went down for breakfast at around 9.30 a.m. and the two girls were in the kitchen grinning from ear to ear, teasing their mother. Where the husband was while all this was going on, I have no idea; he did not appear until about 2 p.m., just before we left the house.

We arrived at the wedding and the wife of my host introduced me to several people, included a number of ladies. As always, the introduction was in Dutch so I did not have a clue what she was saying to them, although I was getting some very strange yet interesting looks.

One particular lady pursued me all evening. She was of

similar age to me, with a very petite frame, black eyes, dark hair and brown skin. She was not a muluto but her colouring gave me the impression she was of mixed race. She also had a very good figure: slim but with a little bit of meat on her, with a nicely shaped bust. She wore glasses and her hair was up in some form of bun. In the evening, after having explored the venue, I decided (with some heavy persuasion from the alcohol in my system) to no longer resist temptation to this lady and take the opportunity to look after her. I found a place underneath the stage of the main hall – with the noise of the disco on the stage, no one would be able to hear or see us there.

She did not need any encouragement as I lead her down some stairs that took us underneath the stage. When we arrived under the stage she told me she was 34, and that her husband was four years older and working in Germany. She admitted to me that she had been deprived of any sexual attention for three months, when he was last home. She also added that he was drunk most of the time, leaving her unsatisfied. She was extremely promiscuous and if she had had her way we would have been there a lot longer than I was expecting. She actually made me very nervous (which was unusual for me) in case someone missed us – I did not want to offend anyone.

We did, however, arrange to meet again the following day for dinner at her house. As soon as I walked through the door I was quickly given a conducted tour around the house, which stopped abruptly when we reached her bedroom. We had a very active session before dinner, although she did want second helpings after we had coffee. This lady, amongst other things, introduced me to many different toys, which it appeared she could not get enough of. I remember going back to my hotel the next day absolutely knackered and very tender in certain areas.

When I returned to Slough it was still necessary for me to attend all the technical courses that the training school provided for the dealer network, to enable me to learn more and have a better understanding of the product.

At the end of my training period I was given a week to assess my department and I was upset, to say the least, to find it in a financial mess. At the interview, Emile had told me that the workshop was operating well and I would not have to make any changes. I only knew how to run a profitable workshop, so I found it very hard to be told that I did not have to make a profit but only to break even. My assessment told me that the department was overstaffed by some 25%, which was around 12 people, and when I presented my report on the department I made this point very strongly to the directors concerned.

About three months later, after I had the opportunity of analysing the monthly accounts over several months' worth, I realized that there was approximately 1,000 hours of unproductive time each month. This was a complete loss and very expensive for the company, and something I felt I must look at with some urgency. I also had a staff consisting of very mixed cultures; English, French, Muslims and some Hindus. The Muslims and the Hindus seemed to cause a lot of friction amongst all the staff and the two races would often fight in the workshop.

At this stage, I felt it necessary to put a redundancy plan together that would take into account the last people in to the department, which I hoped would include the troublemakers. So, I recommended to the managing director and the service director that we make a minimum of 15 people redundant in order to balance the books.

The MD did not take too kindly to this and said that I should reconsider. He informed me that head office in Paris had just made some 6,000 Moroccans redundant within the production factories. They had given them the 6,000 francs each to return to Morocco, which in turn had given the company some very bad publicity in France. The MD made it quite clear to me that he did not approve of my plan and wanted me to take another look at the situation.

I was not happy with the response I received, especially as they would put nothing in writing to me. I felt that if I did not pursue my decision, it might well be my head on the block, with the company asking me to leave as a result of not doing what was expected of me. Maybe I had been brought into the company to slim it down, but the company did not make any suggestions of this during my interviews.

So, I continued writing memorandums to both the MD and the service director, and after about four months they relented and I was given the OK to proceed, despite the reluctance from the personnel department, who had to put the whole thing into operation. However, I presented my plan to the personnel director and a couple of weeks later, it was executed and 15 people were made redundant.

Just before the plan was carried out, I sat down with all the supervisors and explained the situation to them and my reasoning behind it. They took it very hard but most of them understood the action I was taking and agreed that it was necessary.

What with the company being a relatively small one, word got around very quickly and the redundancies did not go down too well. The rest of the staff, as you can imagine, labelled me the scum of the company for making all these people redundant. I had a very quiet couple of weeks as many of the staff sent me to Coventry and it was a few days before they started to speak to me again or sit with me in the staff restaurant. The employees with whom I really expected to have problems were those working in the restaurant; however, they were the only ones that were sympathetic.

I always said that when my name was written on the toilet wall with all the other obscenities, I knew I had made a name for myself in some way or another. One thing I did not expect was that it appeared so soon after me joining the company. One morning, my foreman, John Eaton, advised that I had better go and look at the toilet wall. When I arrived there I saw my name along with some obscenities written on the wall and I started to laugh. John could not understand it as he thought I would be furious; he knew that I had quite a temper when I saw red or when someone crossed me.

I decided to leave the obscenities there for a while, and

about three months later I spoke with the maintenance department. I asked them to decorate the toilet block and smarten it up with new appliances, which went down very well with the staff.

After the redundancies, I immediately set myself a new goal and that was to turn the workshop around within the next five years from a net loss to a healthy profit. I knew that the directors had their eye on me to see if my recent decision on redundancies was a correct one, and knew that if I did not perform, then my head would most definitely be the next to fall.

To my surprise, it only took me four years to achieve this goal, turning the company round to a healthy profit of £500,000. This gave me a tremendous opportunity to invest in equipment that I might never have otherwise had. So in October, when I was doing my budgets, I planned for quite a lot of new equipment to bring the workshop up to date. Emile loved this, and always wanted to be involved while I looked for new equipment. I did not mind and used it to my advantage, always convincing him that the piece we chose was his choice, so he never objected to buying.

One day, I suggested to Emile that the workshop was not laid out as well as it could have been and he threw himself into helping me reorganize the area. Because he and I agreed on the reorganization, I did not have any problem getting the finance authorized to make the changes I wanted. He had one of the administration managers draw up some plans for the workshop, including specifically positioned new equipment, and together we set about redesigning the layout. We also involved a couple of the senior mechanics in the planning as we felt it important to have their input in order to gain their trust and cooperation.

As our parent company used Inmont paint as original equipment on the production lines, I had no option but to honour the existing agreement that was in place in the paint shop at Slough. Our supplier of Inmont was H.T. Wells, a commercial subsidiary of the Inmont Paint Company. Their representative was Jack (surname I cannot remember) and he would come in once a week and replenish the stock we had used through the previous seven days. No one had kept a check on him and over the years we had built up more stock than we needed. There was also a fair bit of old stock that was almost past its sell-by date, so we agreed that we would cleanse the stock and bring it down to the levels that we required.

I also had the backing of the paint manufacturer, which was based in Wolverhampton, and the technical representative that looked after all the manufacturers was Ray Fitchett. In the technical laboratory was a chemist called Janice whom we would call if we had any mixing or colour problems. In the marketing department was a guy called Ian Hobday. As it turned out, all three were to become very good friends of mine, and I am pleased to say that today we still communicate and meet up whenever we can.

Each year, Ray and I would organize a fun day on a Saturday, and he would use a minibus to transport his staff and their partners to Slough. I would organize an afternoon of squash as Ray and I were keen players, and in the evening we would play skittles, followed by a meal in the basket to complete the day. I have to admit that all the squash players from Inmont were extremely good and always won. The skittles were a different matter as it depended on which team had drunk the most, obviously letting the other side win, which was invariably Citroën as most of us had to drive home. They were always very enjoyable events and each year I had people queuing up from all departments to join in.

I remember after one of these events, Ian and his wife were staying with my wife and I and another couple that lived nearby. We were planning on sharing a taxi, but as there were six of us we had to order two. All the girls went in one with the plan for the guys to follow when the second taxi arrived. As it turned out, we arrived home first and we put it down to the erratic driving of our driver, who drove at break-neck speeds through the town. When the girls arrived, it appeared that they had got a puncture and the driver did not have a clue how to change the wheel and the girls had to show him. When they did finally arrive at our house, the driver wanted to charge them nearly twice as much as we had paid, and when the girls refused he got quite upset. He wanted to call the police so we agreed and dialled the number. Well, then the guy took off, leaving us to assume that he was obviously unlicensed.

Back in the office, I frequently got involved in training staff from other countries or from the other Citroën-owned dealerships. The company was, at the time, purchasing dealerships that were in financial difficulties in strategic locations or major cities. If it was a new dealership, then the service managers would come to the training school for the dealer network and undertake a different course each week. When they were not attending school, depending on the job they had within the dealership, they would come to my domain and I would place them with a guy in the workshop, or they would sit in with my administration team, or I would go through the company procedures and endeavour to pass on my management skills to them.

Two of these people stick in my mind as I trained them for a period of three months. The first is George Papadakis from Nicosia, who was the service manager for Cyprus. We became exceptionally good friends and I even spent several holidays in Cyprus and have many fond memories of such enjoyable days and evenings with George and his wife, Eleanor. They had two lovely children – Loucas and Aliki – and Loucas came to Citroën for work experience some years later for three months. I remember that Aliki was very much into Formula 1 and a big fan of Michael Schumacher. I am proud to say that we all still communicate with each other to this very day some 30 years later.

The other person was Jim Corbett from Citroën Glasgow. The company had just acquired the Glasgow dealership and Jim was appointed as service manager. The plan was for Jim to spend three months at Slough with the training school and my administration department. When the workshop reopened in Glasgow after a refurbishment, I was to spend a week with Jim and his staff and hopefully guide them in the right direction. Jim was an excellent communicator with both staff and clients. I built up a good relationship with many of the staff in Glasgow, and later, when I worked in

Fleet, it worked in my favour as they always supported me with any client that had a major problem.

Jim spent some time in Kuala Lumpur with Citroën, and when Jim was over there and I was in Scotland, his wife Yvonne and I would always go out for a meal at one of the famous Asoka Indian restaurants in Glasgow.

I am very pleased to say that Jim and his wife became very close friends of mine over the years, and again we still communicate with each other today. Unfortunately, Jim is currently not enjoying the best of health, but he is a real fighter and I know he will outlive me.

Having brought the workshop at Slough up to date with equipment, my next priority was to computerize the service, paint shop and parts departments, as many of the dealers had already computerized their premises, making us look very inferior. We were, after all, the head office for the UK, so I felt it was a must that we kept up to date with progress and I decided that this was the right time to do it. Emile, my boss, was not computer literate so this immediately gave me a huge disadvantage as he did not think it necessary. However, the assistant aftersales manager, Jim Collis, was extremely knowledgeable on computers and he supported me all the way, eventually persuading Emile that it was the right way to go.

So together, Jim and I looked at various systems that were already in the dealerships. Whilst I was looking for a system that would suit my department at Slough, Jim searched for software that would be suitable for the dealer network and a system that could be recommended by Citroën UK Ltd.

As I did not have a budget in place for this, we had to justify our plan to the MD and the aftersales director who gave us all kinds of excuses as to why we could not do this. Once again, I kept plugging away at the MD and Emile. About three months later the MD stopped me in the corridor to tell me that he had secured the money I wanted for the computerization project. I asked him what Emile thought of this, as I expected a bit of grievance from him, and he replied that Emile did not know yet but I was not to worry and that he would take care of Emile.

So, at that point I started to research different programs that would be suitable for the workshop as well as the dealer network. Jim suggested that I look at a program being developed by Kalamazoo, one which was being updated and would be very suitable for the dealer network.

Firstly, Jim and I went to see a similar system in operation at Warwick Wright's Peugeot dealership in Birmingham. We liked it, but felt that the system needed several enhancements. Kalamazoo assured us these enhancements would be integrated into the new system that was currently being updated, and that the final product would be exceptionally good.

This new program, which was to be called Motodata, was eventually launched and it was agreed that Citroën UK Ltd. and two of its biggest dealers were to pilot the scheme prior to it being recommended and sold to the Citroën dealer network.

As manager of the department, I was expected to manage the whole system, which involved the parts and service departments. So, over the next few weeks I spent a great deal of time in Birmingham at Kalamazoo, learning all the areas of the system.

All the equipment was ordered and delivery was promised within six weeks. When it arrived, I was busy undergoing different training courses at Kalamazoo in Birmingham. The equipment was installed in the relevant places over a couple of weeks. Several of my staff also underwent training on the sections that they were involved with, and I was asked by Kalamazoo to put some plans together as to how I wanted it to go live.

I decided that the simplest way was to go live with Parts and Service together, as it would cause too many problems within our system to only do it in half measures. Most people thought I was raving mad – including Kalamazoo – but I felt it was the only way and the right thing to do. The other dealers that were piloting decided to start with their parts departments.

All the arrangements were made and a date was set with our representative from Kalamazoo, who would be in attendance on that first day of the system going live to ensure that everything ran smoothly. Well, the day before we went live I received a call from Kalamazoo saying that their support guy would not be with us, as he had to be elsewhere. I was not too happy with this, to say the least, and I objected very strongly. However, my reaction made no difference as he was acting on instructions from his management.

I decided to take action and called the MD of Kalamazoo. I asked him if he and his company were really interested in the Citroën business, as it appeared that they were not. From our point of view it was not a good start as they had vowed that someone would be with us for support and guidance when we went live with their system. I suggested if he wanted to keep our business, then he would get someone down there in the morning to support us as promised. Ten minutes later I had a call from the Motadata manager to say that someone would be with me at around ten in the morning. Once again, my popularity was not good in Kalamazoo, but they never crossed me again and I did not lose any sleep over it.

D-day arrived and everything kicked off perfectly. That is, until a tanker arrived at 11.30 a.m. to clean out the catch tanks on the car wash, which caused a tremendous stench. The personnel from the council workshop next door had phoned the emergency services saying there was a major gas leak somewhere and they thought it was coming from Citroën UK.

Consequently, the fire crews arrived from all directions and they decided that the premises were to be evacuated while the gas technicians checked the premises from top to bottom. We all evacuated the building at around 12 noon and they did not let us back in until 2 p.m., when they concluded there was no gas leak and that my explanation regarding the catch tanks causing the smell was, in fact, correct.

Amid all this disruption I felt a bit guilty about the guy from Kalamazoo, who had arrived at 11 a.m. only to be evacuated at 12 p.m.; so I took him for lunch returning at 1.30 p.m., and he left Slough at 3.30 p.m. The launch went superbly, with almost no problems whatsoever. I did, however, spend a few late nights there producing reports until I got the hang of it. In conjunction with Kalamazoo, I devised a program to write all the reports that I needed to be produced overnight. Eventually, over the following two years, all 240 Citroën dealers installed Motadata into their Parts, Service and Accounts departments. As you can imagine, if any dealers had a problem with the program or wanted to do something a bit different, they would ring me for assistance.

Over the next few months I became so proficient on the system that I became an expert. The staff from Motadata would telephone me, wanting to know how I overcame certain problems that they were experiencing. During the course of managing the system, I found several short-cuts that I could use while the system was up and running, rather than get everybody to log out to enable me do what I wanted. Motadata staff told me that this was not possible — but I was able to prove to them that it was and that it was not detrimental to the system.

At around this time, I was invited to a meeting with the BBC regarding building them a new camera car for their horse-racing programme. Their existing car was based on a Citroën DS21 Estate car and it had proved so good over the years that they decided to do the same on a Citroën 2.5 CX Estate. This necessitated working very closely with the technical department of the BBC, and every Friday a planning meeting was attended by all management involved. This was always held at the BBC's technical department at Wembley.

Once the model had been decided upon, it was ordered from production, which took about four weeks as it was classed as a 'special priority' vehicle. After a discussion with my foreman, we decided on the best person to build this vehicle, who promptly set about stripping the interior of the car. The power train, the suspension and the steering all remained standard.

A platform was made and fitted to the roof along with a secure chair for the cameraman to sit, plus a sturdy pillar for the camera to rest on. Once it was almost complete, the car was sent to the technical specialists who fitted all the equipment needed for outside broadcasting.

After all the camera equipment was fitted, I remember having to take the vehicle down to a company on the south coast to have some specialist work done to the equipment. As the vehicle was, at this stage, worth around £90,000, I had to ring the insurance company to get a special policy raised to cover both the equipment and myself. They were very reluctant to give me coverage, but after numerous discussions they agreed. The main problem was that the vehicle was going to be parked on my drive overnight; I got over this by agreeing to park two cars behind it so that it was impossible to get the camera car out of my driveway.

The following morning, I drove the vehicle to the engineering company involved and caught the train back to

Slough. A week later, the vehicle was returned to us for some final fittings. The BBC was delighted with its new vehicle and they continued to use it for the following eight years.

My relationship with the aftersales director, Emile, was a love-hate relationship, and I experienced many rows with him in front of the whole staff. One particular Monday morning, he had decided to have a real go at me, not realizing that I was suffering from Monday morning blues. I was in disbelief as he started his rant towards me, and had chosen to do so in front of all my staff. In return, I let him have it with both barrels, asking him what sort of director bollocked his management in front of the whole workshop. He was gobsmacked and the whole workshop came to a standstill, thinking I had gone over the top. My closing statement to him was that if he wanted to bollock me then he must do so in either my office or his. With that, I walked away from him to my office and he promptly followed me, continuing to tear me off a strip as if nothing had happened. Just before lunch he called me to his office, where the bollocking continued; it became very heated and he actually stated that he was fully aware that I wanted to hit him at that stage. This was very true; although he did not quite realize how close I was to actually thumping him, with only my self-control to hold me back.

When I left his office, I was furious and went straight to the canteen for lunch. I wasn't aware that many of the staff in the company had heard about the incidents. However, this became apparent when several of them made the point of warning me to be very careful as Emile was very hot-headed, and had a reputation for dismissing people that stood up to him.

About ten minutes later, I suddenly felt a hand on my shoulder – it was Emile. He invited me to join him in the directors' dining room and told me that all had been forgotten. Emile admitted to me at a later date that no one had ever spoken to him like that before, and it made him realize that he was in the wrong.

The following day I had a telephone call from his son – Emile had obviously been discussing the incident at home – and he congratulated me for having stood up to his father, who had admired this and told him that he would make me the best service manager in Citroën.

About six months later, I was asked to visit Amsterdam to do an appraisal of Citroën's paint shop, as they wanted to standardize their body shops across the organization in Europe, and head office in Paris had decided that I was the man to do it.

Yes, you are one step ahead of me now ... the same foreman was still there and he said that when he told his family that I was coming over to Amsterdam again, they insisted that I stay with them for the four days of my visit.

As you can imagine, I was delighted with the plan and made a point of being prepared this time, which proved to be a godsend. I often wondered whether the husband knew what was going on. I am convinced that he did, as I knew he had a lady friend from head office with whom he spent a lot of time.

About three months later, I had a call from the twins saying that they were coming to England and would like to come and see me. By pure luck, my wife and I were going to be in Tenerife on holiday, so we were not able to meet up with them. I am not sure how I would have explained that one …

In 1987, I took up playing golf and was introduced to it by a very close friend of mine, Ian Hobday, whom I mentioned earlier. Ian had been promoted to managing director of H.T.Wells, which was now trading under the name of 'Europaints'.

I had organized a session with the golf pro at a local public golf club, and after some tuition we played nine holes. From thereon, Ian and I never stopped playing the game and often met up for a crafty round somewhere. We did improve, however, I never managed to get my handicap below 21 in the UK. Ian would often book a course close to Potters Bar and us guys would play golf while the ladies went off shopping. We would meet up later for a meal and maybe stay over with Ian and his wife.

It was around this time when my second marriage was in trouble; we had both grown apart due to having totally different interests. It was not long after this that I started seeing a lady from Citroën, whose marriage had also broken down, and we had a couple of romantic weekends together. We decided to rent a mobile home in Winkfield Row just outside Windsor, which was convenient for Slough. Shortly after moving there we decided to buy the unit and we eventually moved in together.

After about three months, I decided to give my marriage a second chance. My wife and I agreed that I move back into our home in Kidlington, just outside Oxford, in a bid to make a go of saving our marriage. Four months in, my wife stated that I was the only one that had to change; she had no intention of changing her ways, even though it was some of her ways that had caused our marriage to break down in the first place. It was then that I decided it was not going to work, and after several discussions I moved back into the mobile home at Windsor.

The Health and Safety regulations were always changing in the workshop and paint shop environment, and in that particular year the paint shop had to have certain equipment installed to meet the new regulations along with the deadlines that had been set.

One of the specifics required was a completely separate paint-mixing room, which had to be fireproof to house all the mixing machines and a work bench for the painter to mix the paint colours. We had two mixing machines, so I had to have a reasonably big room; I had been looking at a couple made by different manufacturers and could not make up my mind.

I made a telephone call to the MD of Europaints and asked for his opinion on the two rooms that I was thinking about. Ian phoned me back and reminded me of the promotion that he was currently running: if you spent £10,000 with his company over a period of six months, they would pay for an all-inclusive holiday to Cyprus in a 5-star hotel for one week. He stated that I had already spent £6,000, so if I purchased the mixing room from his company at a cost of £6,500 I would qualify for the trip to Cyprus. I could also extend the holiday for an extra week and pay just £200. I had to go for it, as it was a superb opportunity for my wife and I to go on this trip.

The trip included one week in May staying at the Elias Country Club Hotel in Limmasol, Cyprus. During the week there were several activities organized, such as a trip to the main brewery in Cyprus, a visit to the Tombs of the Kings, and a boat trip from Limmasol to Patras, which took all morning and finished with a barbeque on the beach and then a coach trip back to the hotel.

I had already met the marketing manager of Europaints, John Finnett, but we had not yet met his wife, Carol, until then. These two lovely people were on the same trip and were of a similar age to my wife and I, and we spent many hours with them during the two weeks.

I also contacted my friend in Cyprus so that we could meet up, but he went one better by asking me if I would like to borrow a car while I was there. Of course, I said yes, and he supplied me with a BMW 5 series for the duration of the stay. We took Ian and his wife to their house in Nicosia for dinner during the second week of our stay.

A few months later, John and Carol introduced us to the Costa Blanca, Spain, as they owned a villa close to Altea. We visited them a couple of times and I fell in love with the area. They then suggested that we have a set of keys and visit whenever we wanted, obviously checking with them to make sure it was vacant. These were some great holidays in a great location and a lovely villa. John and Carol also brought another villa in Altea Hills. They kept their first villa and rented it out, but eventually sold it when John retired and they moved to Spain in 2007. Sadly, they both passed away before I completed this book.

Exhibitions

One of my responsibilities was to prepare cars for the motor shows each year. This involved a detailed inspection of all the cars with regards to both the paintwork and the interior. It was necessary to rectify any area that was questionable; this could take a number of weeks depending on each problem. Occasionally, it was necessary to check the underside of the vehicles for damage or imperfections as some stands had mirrors on the floor, showing the underside of the vehicle – it had to be perfect. For the major exhibitions it was possible that one would have to prepare up to 18 vehicles.

Once all the cars and vans were completed and ready for a show, I would then arrange for them to be transported to the venue, for example, either Earls Court in London or the N.E.C in Birmingham. The event organizer would keep in touch with me whilst the contractors were erecting the stand, avoiding the vehicles being delivered too early or too late. Now this in itself caused its own problems, as it was impossible to position vehicles on a stand if the whole stand had not been completed. The contractors were never too happy if the cars arrived before the stand was finished, as they would have to clear the stand to make room to get the vehicles onto it.

I was then expected to position the cars onto the exhibition stand in accordance to a plan that was always supplied by the marketing department. I worked very closely with Marketing and it was necessary to have the stand up and running at 6 a.m. on the morning of Press Day.

Once the cars and vans were positioned, I had to abide by the safety regulations relating to vehicles in an exhibition centre. Some of these were that all the fuel tanks had to be drained of petrol or diesel, which had to be done in the workshop before the cars left. One litre of fuel would be injected just before the vehicle left the premises. This would normally be sufficient, running out by the time they were positioned on the stand.

Batteries had to be disconnected, handbrakes locked and suspension blocked on the hydro-pneumatic vehicles. This was important as the hydro-pneumatics tended to sink over a couple of days and the blocks kept them at the ride-height position. Once these were done, it was a major operation to reposition a vehicle if the directors decided that they did not like the layout. As it was, at the end of Press Day we would move the cars around and place two or three more on the stand.

On one particular occasion, we arrived at the N.E.C. only to find that the French contractors were three days behind, and we could not get the cars onto the stand. As it was impractical to leave the cars outside for three days and nights, it was decided that we would position them in the gangways around the stand. As you can imagine, this did not go down too well with the contractors or the exhibition organizers, and I hoped and prayed that the vehicles would not get damaged.

Eventually, the stand was completed at about 5 p.m. before the show was due to open the following day. We then set to work positioning the 18 vehicles on the stand, working through the night and completing the task at around six in the morning, four hours before the exhibition opened. In order for us to have done this we had to get special dispensation from the organizers' office and the security of the N.E.C. to allow us to be on the premises overnight. This, however, was not difficult, as invariably it meant that you had to put your hand in your pocket and give someone a large back-hander, but it always worked. It reminded me very much of South America.

Fleet Manager

After my reorganization of the workshop, business ran very smoothly and efficiently. It turned out that I was the longest serving workshop manager that Citroën had ever had at Slough, and I had managed to turn the profitability around within four years.

In 1987, the company moved to Bath Road, Slough, and the workshop was closed to the public; its occupation now purely to look after the company fleet, which, of course, included the press cars.

I appreciated that there was not space at the Bath Road site for the workshop to continue as it was, but I was disappointed that the company should just dismiss the fact that we were contributing £500,000 to the company's profitability. I was reminded by the directors that the company was in the business of distributing cars through the dealer network, and not of repairing cars.

In 1988, I was appointed Company Fleet Services Manager, looking after the company fleet, transport department, workshop, and parts department. I had a total workforce of 40 staff and 1,200 cars and vans on the fleet. The fleet was made up of company cars, press demonstrators, fleet demonstrators, and cars for sale.

To support this we had a preparation centre at the Isle of Sheppey, which prepared all the new vehicles for the company. Very often, Fleet Sales would do a deal with a hire company, where I would be called upon to prepare anything from 200 to 1,000 vehicles over maybe two or three weeks. The preparation centre would handle this and in each case I would negotiate a price per car, which could be affected by the timescale and the quantity.

Unfortunately, the department was disbanded in 1990 due to a reorganization of the company at Bath Road, leaving me in a very precarious position. One director would have liked to see me made redundant, but the aftersales director had other plans lined up for me, although it would take him a few weeks to sort things out. So for the next few weeks I kept my head down and looked busy, visiting the preparation centre more than was necessary.

During this period I also tried keeping myself busy by joining the Citroën Golf Society, which had started the previous year.

The first golf day created numerous difficulties as most of the directors and senior management in the company were non-golfers. The personnel and sales director stated very clearly that under no circumstances were we to hold another golf day during the working week; if we did, it would be considered as gross misconduct and we, as organizers, would have to suffer the consequences as per the company disciplinary procedure. One of the other directors was particularly upset because he thought we should have organized it through the Sports and Social Club as opposed to organizing it under the banner of the Citroën Golf Society.

With the threat of a disciplinary for gross misconduct, you can imagine that this put our backs up, but we were determined that the golf society was going to continue.

So, I made a few enquiries to find a golf club that would take a society booking at the weekends. This actually proved easier than any of us had anticipated and I found several clubs that were more than happy to accommodate us on a Saturday or Sunday afternoon. So I began to organize the next event and realized that there may be a few advantages of going through a social club and getting their approval. I had a discussion with the chairman and asked him if the social club would be willing to adopt the golf society, and he agreed to raise the proposal at the next committee meeting.

A week later, he informed me that the club was more than happy to adopt the Golf Society; however, they stressed that they did not want to be involved in any of the organization. This suited the society perfectly and I went about talking to people for sponsorship. This included the marketing department. I explained that I was organizing a golf tournament for the social club, and would they consider donating some prizes from their accessory section. They, in turn, contacted the chairman and between them they agreed to give me £1,000 worth of prizes of my choice. This sum was to be split between the marketing department and the social club. I considered this to be a great result as prizes played a big part in our costs and we would benefit from any help we could get.

I also contacted a few of the suppliers that I dealt with and set up a sponsorship package. This included £300, which enabled them to enter a team of four – two of which were free of charge, while the other two paid the going rate for the day. It was surprising to find that in most cases I only had to ask these companies and they were more than happy to support us.

In the first two years I organized three tournaments each year for the society; but this put a lot of pressure on me, so I cut it back to two a year, making it much more manageable. However, after about six years my role with Citroën had become increasingly demanding, and I only had time to organize one event a year. This became a charity day, attracting around 90 players with additional guests for the dinner in the evening, which normally hosted 130 people. We always supported the company's chosen charity and each year we would donate around £1,500 to £2,000 to them.

Europaints were our main sponsors each year and they would always enter a team of four players. The MD, Ian Hobday, or an elected member of staff would give an after-dinner speech. Over the years, Europaints donated somewhere in the region of £12,000 to the Citroën Golf Society.

There were many sponsors, most of which were business contacts of mine, that contributed to the society every year. All of them played golf, making it easier to raise sponsorship, and the generosity of these sponsors never ceased to amaze me.

It was around this time when I was contacted by Ian's wife, Helen, who was planning a surprise party for his 30th birthday. She wanted me to entertain Ian during the day so that the ladies could prepare the house and the food. There was going to be around 40 people attending this party, so they wanted him out of the house by 10 a.m. and I was not to return with him until around 7.30 p.m. Well, I managed this with ease and organized a round of golf at the Hatfield and London Country Club. After the game, we all showered and had a snack in the bar when one of the lads – a neighbour of Ian's – suggested we went to the snooker club in Hatfield, which was a great idea as it was too early to return to his house. The only problem was we were having so much fun that it proved very difficult to get Ian away to return to his home by the time instructed by Helen.

When we arrived at the house it was full of people, and Ian was quite taken back by it all, then realizing that I was part of the plan. Later on in the evening, one of his work colleagues had organized a strippergram. When she arrived, it was clear she was a Roly Poly lady. Ian's wife (who did not know about this) was mortified and not at all happy, telling the person that had organized it to promptly get rid of her as she did not want her in the house.

Six weeks after the closure of my department, Citroën appointed me as their fleet service manager, and the territory that I was given covered the whole of the UK, including Northern Ireland. This seemed one hell of a task, but I decided to give it a whirl and see where it took me, particularly as I did not have too many other options at that time.

The main advantage of the job was that no one had done it before me, so I did not have any act to follow. Another advantage was that while I was on the road I was my own boss, and no one seemed to trouble me at all. As you can imagine, a territory as big as this meant an awful lot of traveling was involved, which at first I did not object to.

After a while, though, it became very apparent that I had to manage my time as effectively as possible. More often than not, I would go into the office on a Monday morning for a couple of hours and then go visiting fleet clients, not returning home until Thursday evening. I endeavoured to avoid the roads on a Friday, as the traffic was always bad on a Friday afternoon. So I planned this as my administration day.

Life in fleet could be very pleasant, as most of the fleet managers I came into contact with were extremely nice people. It was very important to have a good rapport with them as it made my life easier and the heat was never turned on me unless I failed to produce the goods. The best part of the job was that no two days were the same.

There were lots of perks with the job, including many hospitality events that included product launches of new vehicles, golf days and exhibitions. I always maintained that with these events I could meet maybe 20 or 30 clients under one roof in one day, which could take me approximately one month to visit them all, taking logistics into consideration. As a result, the fleet department always invited me to attend most of the events.

I was also invited to attend golf days or corporate days organized by my clients, some of which were very memorable, and quite often I took a day's holiday if I was unable to justify a day out of the office.

I am going to change direction at this point, as I think the next subject has played a very important role in my life. We will come back to fleet at the end of this chapter.

Corporate Entertaining

It was because of all these hospitality events that I became interested in corporate entertaining, and through various contacts I managed to set up my own company, which I called 'D & S Golf Matters'. I talked to my director about this and he had no objection, as long as it did not interfere with my work.

I had a contact at Pringle, so we had some red polo shirts embroidered with a logo that had been designed by another contact of mine. I started to capitalize on the experience that I had gained from the Citroën events, so I began to organize several events through contacts and friends that I had gathered over the years.

I think the first event I did was a golf day for Dupont Paint Company, and Ray Fitchett was the organizer at Dupont. I arranged a meeting with him at the Hatfield and London Golf Country Club, which I thought would be perfect for them. We gave Ray a tour of the facilities, and he was more than happy for the company's first event to be held there. The golf club was Japanese-owned and was not a difficult course; but it was quite a long course that always tested the irregular golf player. I hired Roger Mace, a golf professional, to do a demonstration of golf shots and give an after-dinner speech.

I also hired two very lovely, professional ladies who usually worked on the Honda exhibition stand. I utilized these ladies for the registration of the golfers, who were all clients of

Dupont, and then to organize and escort them to wherever they should be next, be it on the first tee or in the restaurant. The ladies really went down well with all the guys with their very bubbly and chatty personas, and whenever I met one of their clients at a later date, they always asked for their phone numbers.

The format of the day was registration at 8 a.m. with coffee and bacon rolls, with the first tee-off time scheduled for 8.30 a.m. As they came off the 18th hole, the ladies ushered the golfers into the pro-shop where they were invited to take part in a simulated tee-shot competition. The computer was set at 165 m (181 yards) over water, and the nearest to the pin won a bottle of champagne. The ladies did not let them hang around for too long as lunch was being served, followed by Roger Mace's demonstration before returning to the course for another 18 holes.

The event was so successful that Ray asked me to do another golf day for him the following year. This we did, making one or two changes to improve the day as we had both realized that we had tried to fit too much in on the first occasion. We did not want to change the ladies, but one of them could not attend the second event so I chose another with the same qualities: good looks, a perfect figure, and a personality to go with both.

Then another friend approached me: Ian Hobday, managing director of Europaints, now part of the BASF Group. Ian had recently done a corporate event at 24 Hours of Le Mans, and it had been a disaster for him as they had hired a Winnebago motorhome. It had not gone too well as, firstly, no one wanted to do any driving, cooking or cleaning. So, it all fell on Ian. He asked me if I would be interested in taking on the event for the following year. I admitted to him that I had never done anything like it before, but if he had faith in me, then I would be more than happy to take the job on.

My briefing was to do a similar thing as he had done, but to have four 6-berth motorhomes with at least two of them benefitting from awnings. He also said that he would like me to keep within the budget of £10,000.

After some research, I found a company in the Forest of Dean that rented out motorhomes, and after visiting them I decided to book four for the weekend of the event, which was always around the third week of June. The plan was to leave on the Wednesday evening using the P&O ferry from Portsmouth, arriving early in the morning in Le Harvre, then drive to a small town about an hour from the port to stop for breakfast. We would then push on in the hope of arriving at the circuit at around 4 p.m., stopping en route at a supermarket to stock up with food, wine, and beer. Finding your site was always a pain because there were so many entrances, and the officials had the ability to send you to all of them. Over the years, we got more familiar with the way the French worked, becoming as cunning as them. On two occasions, we actually parked on a site right next to the paddock, which was not shown on our entrance ticket or on the locations on the circuit plan; but because we were early no one took any notice.

We would ignore the parking instructions from organizers and arrange the four motorhomes to our preference, usually in a square with a canopy from one of them to cook under, should it rain. On our first visit, we were on a campsite and the location was not good as it was quite a distance from the circuit. However, the atmosphere on this site was tremendous, particularly in the evenings as we watched the different gatherings gradually getting drunk. Everyone joined in with the singing, no matter what their nationality or how crude the songs were.

Our location that first year was not good as we had ended up on a campsite. I did some research and made a few enquiries for a better pitch, in the event of being asked to repeat the event the following year.

I also did all the cooking for the group: 16 in total, including myself. This consisted of three cooked meals a day, including a full English breakfast, a light lunch, and a hot meal or a barbeque in the evening. As you can imagine, I did not see much of the racing – when I was not cooking, I was recovering with my feet up, preparing myself for the next meal.

Breakfast was never a problem as the group was never awake very early following a highly-charged evening with alcohol. That gave me the opportunity to get cracking, so when they emerged one-by-one, breakfast was always ready.

Lunch was normally a cold buffet, and I was usually well-prepared, as Ian and I had agreed menus beforehand. We had brought a lot of food with us from the UK, which I had purchased from a cash and carry that specialized in catering, reducing my workload considerably.

Then there were the evening barbeques. At first, I have to admit that my timings were way out, so some of the lads helped me out. The fact I was running a bit late meant that many of them were well on their way to being pissed before I even served dinner. I tried to do something different every night, and eventually my timings were perfect. By the end of the event, I was happy with the catering side of things and pleased with what I had accomplished.

We left the track at about 4.30 p.m. on the Sunday and drove back to Le Harvre to find a parking slot as close to the ferry as we could. Boarding was at 7 a.m. so we hoped our parking would not cause a problem staying there overnight. It was not difficult to find a restaurant willing to accommodate 16 people for dinner. As usual, most of the party had consumed quite a lot of drink, so when they turned in for the evening, they all slept like babies.

I remember that first year when I got home at around 9 p.m. I was so knackered and said if I had the opportunity to do it again, I would have to have someone help me with the catering and general duties.

Well, I was asked to do it again; in fact, I did it for the next eight years, getting more professional each year and using more and more equipment. On the second year, I had brought a much bigger BBQ with a lid that turned it into an oven, so I could be more ambitious with what I cooked. I had also acquired a canopy, which was 3.5 sq. m and, with one of the motor homes having a canopy as well, we were always prepared for the worst weather. The BBQ and the canopy were always shown on the invoice as equipment hired, which helped cover the cost of these items. Ian also supplied a couple of ladies from the office to assist me with the catering.

The downside to all this professionalism was that Ian would always put me to the test at some point during the event. I remember on one occasion he had been at the track in the morning. He came back and said he had met a group of his clients and had invited them back for dinner in the evening. Fortunately, on this particular evening, I had a curry on the menu, so I just had to prepare a bit more to cater for the eight extra mouths.

He did this on numerous occasions, and I remember the worst was when he informed me that there would be an extra twelve for dinner. On this particular night, we had planned a barbeque, so I asked one of the lads that had come on his Harley Davidson if he could go into town and buy some chicken portions and sausages. When he returned, he said he could not find chicken portions, so instead brought me four whole chickens. This gave me a lot more work, having to cut them into portions before I could cook them. I always seemed to manage and get through it without too many problems, purely because I came to expect it and always went prepared to cater for extras without much difficulty.

The last Le Mans 24 Hours that I did, I hired a large coach that belonged to a Dutch guy that I had met at one of the corporate days somewhere with Citroën. The interior of the coach was designed with a galley, toilet, and 16 armchairs, each facing a large television screen. Whilst travelling, you could watch a video, and when stationary, you could erect a satellite dish that you wound up and pointed in a direction that would get the best signal. This particular facility was very useful at Le Mans, picking up the local channel providing national coverage of the event.

Ton, the owner, and a Dutch friend of mine, would always load the coach up with beer, wine and spirits in Holland, so we got everything at duty-free prices. The party met at Heathrow airport and we flew to Charles de Gaulle airport, just outside Paris. We motored down, staying overnight at a hotel a little farther out than we anticipated, but this was counteracted by leaving 15 minutes earlier than planned in the morning. On the Saturday, we spent the day at the circuit and at midnight we drove back to the hotel. As it was around 1.30 a.m. most of the guys went to bed, while one or two stayed in the coach drinking until 2.30 a.m. when Ton suggested that they went to bed as he had to drive the following morning.

On Sunday, we drove back to the track, arriving at about 11 a.m., and stayed to see the finish before driving back to the hotel just outside of Paris, where we dined and drank exceptionally well before returning to the UK on Monday morning.

I organised somewhere in the region of 15 corporate days and the last one really put me to the test. It was the European Championship in June 2000. Ian said to me that he really fancied doing a trip to a group game in Charleroi,

Belgium. So we sat down and mapped out a plan to fly everyone from Heathrow to Brussels. I would meet them there with Ton's coach, which Ton would have already loaded up with wine, spirits and beer. The drive to the stadium would take approximately two hours, and we planned to have dinner in a restaurant before collecting our entry tickets. After the match, we would return to the same restaurant for a buffet before taking the coach back to Brussels, where we would stay overnight in a hotel close to the airport before the flight home.

The day finally came, and I'd planned to catch an earlier flight so I could liaise with Ton and be there to meet the party when they arrived. All went well and Ton and I were in position and waiting for the party's flight to land when I noticed that the arrivals board indicated it had been delayed. I contacted Ian who informed me that apparently all the British Airways computers had crashed at Heathrow and that the airport was at a stand-still, but they hoped to get away by 2 p.m. This did not happen and they were all sat on-board the plane waiting to take off. They eventually departed at 4.30 p.m., which meant that they were going to land at about 5.30 p.m. (our time).

This was cutting it rather fine as we still had a two-hour drive to the stadium, which would now hit rush hour, so we decided we would have to abandon plans to go to the restaurant before the game. I searched the food outlets at the airport and there was nowhere to get a takeaway, except the Pizza Bar. So, at about 5.15 p.m. I ordered 15 pizzas with various toppings. Well, the guy looked at me as if I was mad and insisted I pay for the pizzas before he started cooking them. There was a huge queue and I had created a nightmare for him, but thankfully he served them up within 20 minutes.

I got my Pizzas and the guys arrived, and Ian said that he had met six guys on the plane and had invited them to join us on the coach. Because of the delay we had hit the rush hour in Brussels. It was a nightmare – we crawled out of the city and eventually arrived at the stadium ten minutes after the kick-off.

We were in the upper stand and I remember when England scored – the whole stand was shaking as everyone jumped up and down in celebration, and I have to admit it was quite frightening. From then on, everything went well with a great result from England winning 1-0. After the game, we were able to go to the restaurant as planned for a meal and a few drinks, arriving at the hotel at about 1 a.m.

However, when we got to the airport the following morning, we discovered that most of the flights to Heathrow that day had been cancelled, including mine. The rest of the party was booked onto a British Midland flight. Ian and I approached their desk and explained that one member of our party was no longer travelling with us, effectively leaving a spare seat. Ian requested the airline allocate the seat to me, which, fortunately, they agreed to do. That trip was a fine example that no matter how detailed your plans are, they can always go very wrong when you least expect them to, through no fault of your own; and the one skill you require to cope is the ability to think very quickly on your feet.

Back to Citroën, and after about two years into the job, I had grouped all the companies that Citroën dealt with together, so that if I was in a particular area, I could readily see who else I could pay a visit to. I always worked to a policy that if I had to travel more than 200 miles to see a client, I would stay the night somewhere. This also meant that over a two-day period I would be able to see perhaps five or six other clients, again depending upon their location. This policy allowed me to manage my time more effectively.

Over the years, the travelling and staying in hotels were beginning to get to me and I admit I was not enjoying the job quite as much. However, the job had brought me many memorable events and opportunities. I always enjoyed the corporate days, the fleet exhibitions and especially the golf days with fleet. On many occasions, I was invited by some of the leasing companies to attend their golf days at different venues around the country, which would probably mean staying overnight and ending up in a nightclub or a bar somewhere until the early hours of the morning.

One thing I did find during my travels was that the further north I went, the more hospitable the people were. For instance, in Manchester the principal dealer would always entertain you. In Newcastle, the dealer fleet manager would always take you out along with one of his clients for dinner somewhere and then inevitably end up in a nightclub in town. Newcastle was always a great experience; I had never seen behaviour like it before, with the ladies cavorting on the dance floor in a bid to attract a mate for the evening, regardless of sex.

Then there was Scotland, where the social side of the job became second to none. Firstly, one of the staff at Citroën Glasgow had a connection with Glasgow Rangers, so I always worked it so that I visited Glasgow when there was a home game on, and he never failed to produce a ticket for me. I could be sat anywhere in the ground – the only thing I knew was that I would always be sat with other Glasgow supporters.

When I was not at a match, the staff at the dealership always invited me out and I got to know a lot of people in Glasgow and some I am very proud to say remain very good friends of mine today. The Scottish people are some of the nicest people I have ever met and so generous that they would spend their last penny on you.

During my travels to Leeds, I was visiting a company (Appleyard Contracts, now ING Leasing) and I went into the fleet manager's office; there, pinned up on the wall, were six photographs of me that someone had taken from one of the books previously written by Brian Moylan and Bill Price. I was taken aback as it was totally unexpected. It was then that I thought, "God, I have been recognized …"

Alan Maude, MD of Appleyard Contracts, always invited me to his company golf day with a banquet afterwards. It was always held at a prestigious golf club in the Leeds area and was a very enjoyable day, and one that I always made a point of being available for.

There were, of course, various obstacles throughout my career – I will give you a few examples:

One of our clients had 3,000 Berlingo vans and decided to install roof racks, which they purchased from their local dealer. They had them assembled and the mechanic in each branch had fitted them. However, one of these vans had been travelling through one of the border towns when the roof rack came off. Citroën was immediately called to investigate and I was sent to their head office in Dumbarton to make a few enquiries. Fortunately, I was able to prove that Citroën had not supplied the roof racks, and that the mechanics had not followed the written instructions that were supplied with each roof rack. But in order to capitalize on the situation, I agreed terms to supply them with roof racks for the remainder of the fleet.

On another occasion, I was called to a local council in Scotland that had purchased a number of C25 vans and was experiencing a number of serious problems. During my enquiries, I discovered that the drivers hated them and were doing everything they could to discredit them, including sabotaging a vehicle in an endeavour to persuade the council to go back to purchasing Ford. To help resolve this issue with the management, we agreed for three demonstrators to be given to the council on permanent loan, giving them the facility of a back-up vehicle whenever they had an issue with another. We also arranged for our dealer in Glasgow to give them all the support they needed.

I was also called to a multinational company in Staines, Middlesex that had agreed to buy 6,000 Berlingo vans. Each van was modified by a company on the Isle of Sheppey and I had to set up procedures to enable them to do their own warranty work. It was also necessary to arrange for the local dealer to supply them with parts and accessories. There were several parts that we had to get made especially for them, as some of the modifications involved an enhanced security system. The vans were going to be carrying some very expensive parts, so we had to ensure that the alarm systems would not fail.

I also used to visit all the leasing and rental companies that we dealt with and set up a very close working relationship, so that if they experienced a major problem, they knew who to call for the issue to be resolved.

These are just a few examples, but with some 400 clients all over the UK and with only 'yours truly' representing aftersales and being responsible for good rapport, you can imagine it kept me very busy.

Club Captain

In 1998, I was asked to step in as vice-captain at Richings Park and Country Club, as the existing vice-captain had resigned, leaving the club in a difficult situation. I was one of the founder members of the club and had been there for six years since it opened. I accepted the challenge and had to attend many meetings during the course of the remainder of the year, in preparation for the captaincy the following April. I also had to attend a lot of the club functions, so I knew exactly what was expected of me in my new role.

That year seemed to go very quickly and April came before I was ready, although I knew there were a lot of people around to support me if I got into difficulties with the procedures and formalities of the club.

I officially became captain on 4 April 1999 and immediately started planning my captain's drive-in, which always took place in the first couple of weeks of the captaincy. This, I decided, would be a charity day in aid of multiple sclerosis, as one of the lady members and a friend of mine at the club were sufferers.

I started off with a 'Longest Drive Competition', which everyone paid £1 to enter, and this is where I had my drive-in as captain. On this particular fairway, there was a lake along the right-hand side, and the members were convinced that I would drive into the lake so they had prepared polystyrene boats with flags in them. Fortunately, I hit a perfect ball straight down the middle of the fairway, prompting a huge cheer from all the members present, and I was officially captain for the next twelve months.

After my captain's drive-in, my next big day was the Captain's Day, and the captain was always expected to cover the costs of the day, which would be a format of his choice. This was always one of the most supported days on the fixture list. I had been giving it a lot of thought over the past months and decided to approach one or two of my fleet customers, namely the leasing companies with whom I had a tremendous relationship, to see if I could raise some money and prizes, as most of the managing directors of these companies were very keen golfers.

Well, four of the companies gave me £200 each, which was

a great start as this enabled me to do a bit of bartering with the chef at the club. Every weekend, he offered a three-course Sunday lunch for £5.00, so I asked him to do the same for the members on my day, with a glass of wine thrown in. After numerous discussions with the chef and the owner of the club, we eventually settled for £5.50, which I thought was very good – I had been prepared to pay up to £6.50. This gave me some additional funds to buy other prizes and to organize a raffle, as, once again, the day was to be in aid of the same charity for the benefit of multiple sclerosis sufferers. To make up the deficit of the costs, I charged all the members that entered the competition £4, which was the normal fee for club competitions.

The turnout was tremendous with some 135 members taking part, and it is fair to say that a great day was had by all. I managed to socialize well and had so many drinks bought for me that by the end of the day I was well on my way. With the balance of the sponsorship and the raffle we actually raised £1,400 for the Multiple Sclerosis Society at a nearby centre in Buckingham.

Each year, the PGA organized several competitions for the captains of each club within the UK, and this I did enjoy participating in. Each captain picked his own team of four members of his club, and my team usually included myself and three close friends: Savador Ramayon, Brian Sunden and Shaun O'Donnell. We participated in three competitions around the country at different venues, but unfortunately we did not get past the first round in any of them. However, we played some superb courses and had some great fun participating.

The club professional and I decided to team up and throw a challenge out to all the members to play 18 holes against us, with the losers buying the drinks. Friday afternoon was a good time for me to play this competition as I finished early that day, so we usually teed off at around 4.30 p.m. We put a notice on the members' notice board, and within a couple of days we had 13 fixtures, which just about took us through the light evenings. It always caused a stir in the clubhouse over the weekend as the other members wanted to know how their mates had got on, and who had to buy the beer. As I remember it, we lost 12 matches and drew 1, so we spent quite a lot of money over the bar with many of the members being hard drinkers.

My next major trophy at the club was the President's Cup and, again, we always had a very good turnout for this competition, with my particular year being no exception, with about 110 players participating.

The following month was the club championship, which was held on the Saturday and Sunday. Both days spent on the golf course were always thoroughly enjoyable. Then, there was, of course, the presentation. This took place on the Sunday afternoon, and the weekend would end with celebrations and many beverages had by all.

There were other club competitions during the course of the year, along with the medal competitions at the weekends. These were held between the major competitions, and each event usually attracted around 100 members. They were always held on Saturday or Sunday, alternating each month so those unable to play on a

Saturday could play the following weekend, and vice versa.

One time, I organized a sixties evening and out of the 120 people that attended, I was the only person that dressed up in sixties gear, complete with floppy sleeves and the bell-bottomed trousers that I'd hired for the evening. The owner of the club said that she was surprised I still owned what I was wearing, not realizing that they were, in fact, from somewhere other than my personal wardrobe.

My next big event was an evening function, a presentation night, which consisted of a three-course meal and the presentation of all the club trophies that had been won throughout the year, accompanied by a well-known speaker. The evening would begin rather early in comparison to other functions I'd organised, as the presentation alone would usually take around an hour and a half, what with all the photographs that were taken by the club and the winners' partners. This year my guest speaker was Sandy Jones, chief executive of the PGA. and was based at the Belfry golf club. He had made some very controversial statements a couple of weeks prior to the event in regards to ladies playing golf. Quite a large proportion of the club consisted of women, who inevitably wanted to take him to task about this, but we managed to suppress them somehow or other.

My final event was the AGM, which, of course, I chaired. Unfortunately, two days before the event, the Seniors Club Captain died. I had a private word with his widow, who was present at the event, and asked if she would object to me calling for a minute's silence as a mark of respect for him and his involvement in the club. He, too, had been a founder member and had helped get the club off the ground.

The evening was a great success and the elections went extremely well with no one having to be cajoled into becoming a committee member. The evening concluded with my captaincy of the club and the captain handed his position over to me with the presentation of a set of whisky decanters displayed in a quality wooden frame that bore a brass plaque on the front, declaring the date of my position as captain.

It was, to say the least, a very fulfilling year and one that I will treasure, as it was a great experience and a privilege to have been the club captain of Richings Park Golf and Country Club. My one regret was that my wife did not enjoy the social scene at all, which inevitably put me under a fair degree of pressure at times.

In January of 2003, Citroën decided to change their provider for emergency breakdowns, awarding the new contract to the RAC. Now, we all expected a few teething problems, but the reality was that, as the months went by, the problems escalated beyond our expectations. The fleet sector appeared to be suffering the most and it seemed the RAC operators had no sympathy whatsoever.

Just before I went on holiday in February, I mentioned my concerns to the aftersales director, who suggested that I went along to their monthly meetings with the RAC. The next meeting was scheduled for the following week in his office and he gave me carte blanche to say exactly what I wanted, so long as I was precise and factual.

The day arrived and I asked my boss if I could speak first, as I had another appointment scheduled later that day. The meeting was attended by my director and the operations director, along with the operations manager (who was a very pretty lady) and the development manager from the RAC. Also present was the liaison manager from Citroën. Two of the attendees were female, so I had to curtail my language. Unfortunately, about an hour before the meeting, I had to deal with a case involving our biggest client at the time, BSkyB, who had something in the region of 6,000 vehicles. The RAC had refused point-blank to assist the driver or the company without a £200 deposit and a driver's licence. Fortunately, I managed to resolve the whole situation, but I went into the meeting with all guns blazing.

My boss introduced me and stated that I was not happy, and requested they listen to what I had to say. Well, I laid into all of them explaining that the operating rules that they had implemented and forced upon us were simply not working, and that someone in this room had fucked up big time (which did, however take the pretty smile off the operations manager's face). Whoops, the word just slipped out ... except I did not regret it at all as I felt it described the situation perfectly. I went on to explain that the system might have been working for the retail client, but it certainly was not for the fleet operator, whom I pointed out represented 48% of our business. I also said that no one in the room had taken the trouble to get off their arses and talk to those on the front line of the operations who had to deal with the customers' responses to these changes. If they had bothered, then maybe we would not have found ourselves in the position we were in. I continued to explain a couple of cases in detail and then concluded by repeating that maybe the person or persons that had fucked up would reassess the system, actually talk to the front-liners, and this time incorporate the fleet sector. I left the meeting knowing I had probably pushed my luck to the limits, but I went in there to say what I felt needed saying and that is exactly what I did.

My director told me the following morning that I had pitched my presentation perfectly, and the response was that they had agreed to certain temporary measures to fill in the gaps until they had time to reassess the entire policy covering the fleet operator.

I had left the company by the time the policies had been changed, but I understand that the updated system covering the fleet is working exceptionally well and the people concerned were, I am sure, relieved that they would not have to listen to me again.

I was very fortunate while working for the fleet services, as I always had an exceptional team of people working for me, which enabled me to spend so much time out of the office, building tremendous relationships with all the clients of Citroën UK Ltd. This elevated not only my own capabilities, but also those of the many salesmen to produce the goods expected from the company. I was also fortunate to have had the faith and trust from my direct boss and my director, who left me to do what I did best and get on with it on my own, provided I produced an itinerary each week confirming my plans, and that I brought back the results that they were confident I would achieve.

My Retirement

It was 28 February 2003 and my wife and I were on holiday at our villa in Spain. We had just returned from a lunch with Angela and Alan, who had previously sold us our first property there.

Angela was, at the time, the general manager of a property company and estate agency in Spain, and she made the suggestion that as I was almost sixty years young, I should retire and come and work for her. However, there was a small problem: it was imperative that I started work on 5 May 2003. The company required two months' notice – it was 28 February. I had very little time to make a huge decision and act upon it.

When we returned to our villa, we sat on the terrace with a stiff gin and tonic, contemplating the offer that had just been put to me. Our biggest problem was, of course, Mother, whom by now had lost most of her mobility and been admitted into the Marcham Road Hospital in Abingdon. She was waiting for the family to find her suitable accommodation, as it was not possible for her to return to her warden-controlled apartment at Elainor Court.

We were living in Maidenhead at the time and, being a little out of the way, my brothers took it upon themselves to try and find somewhere for Mother to go. They found that the standards varied greatly and a lot of what they had seen was unhygienic, and would be completely unsuitable. My brother John fortunately knew a lady that was in charge of a new residential home that was being built in Wallingford, near Oxford. He managed to get Mother's name put on the waiting list, but the problem was that the home was not due to be finished for another five months. Marcham Road Hospital was constantly pestering us to find alternative accommodation as quickly as we could, but my brothers managed to stall them and hang on until the preferred rest-home opened.

As I considered my options, I noted that at the end of April I could retire, as I would be 60, meaning the pension fund would not penalize me. I had also been saving the maximum amount in AVC's with Equitable Life, though I was aware that we had lost a percentage in the collapse of the business of Equitable Life. However, I knew that as soon as I was retired, I could go to the open market with the funds I had accumulated to acquire the best annuity that was available to me.

I also took into consideration that it was noticeable that the fleet business was changing rapidly. My director at the time was also putting pressure on me to change certain aspects of the job, including the support that we as a department provided to the fleet sector. I was opposed to the changes he was suggesting and felt that he was letting me get away with it because of my experience. He also appreciated the relationships I had with the majority of the fleet that we were dealing with in big volumes. I was not confident that I would be able to continue to support the fleet as I had been if some of these changes he wanted to impose were implemented. My wife had also stated that she felt I was getting very tired and fed up travelling up and down the motorways, leaving home some mornings at 6 a.m. So, after a lot of pondering and a couple more drinks, I decided that it might well be a very good time to retire.

My wife and I had our house in Maidenhead and the property in Spain, so we did not have to worry about accommodation. We had no debts to worry about either.

Taking all these points into consideration, I realized that if I was to give my two months' notice to Citroën, then I would have to give in my notice that day in order to be able to leave at the end of April. With positive thoughts in front of us, I decided to ring the personnel manager, who I knew very well, and asked him if he would accept my resignation over the phone. He agreed, as long as my letter of resignation was on his desk the day I returned to work. He also suggested that I must have had a fabulous round of golf that day to make such a bold decision while on holiday.

On our return to the UK, my wife and I sat down and had a long chat with Mother, who gave us her blessing to move to Spain – she wanted us to get on with our lives and she did not want to hold us back in any way.

So on 3 May, I flew out to Spain and started work two days later. We had arranged for a friend of ours, Tel – who owned a courier business just outside of Abingdon – to bring all our belongings out to Spain the week my wife arrived.

Having previously loaded the van in Maidenhead, Tel

arrived in Spain a couple of days before my wife, and together we sorted out what we wanted to use straightaway and what would have to be put into storage. The plan was to put our house in Maidenhead on the market and buy a bigger villa suitable for all the family. As a result, we temporarily put all the excess furniture and belongings into a storage depot. The transition of all our belongings went smoothly. The only problem was that Tel had a call from the office with instructions to return to the UK, so unfortunately we were unable to squeeze in a round of golf as planned.

Three months into the new job, I had a phone call from my general manager asking me to meet the proprietor and the accountant at the Nautical Club in Torrevieja on Saturday morning. Unless I was with a client, it was strictly against my religion to work on Saturdays as I considered myself to be semi-retired.

As it was the boss and the accountant who wanted to see me, my immediate thoughts were that they were going to ask me to retire. However, the GM did say that it was to my advantage and said I would be silly not to go and hear what they had to say. After deciding to swallow my pride, I went to the Nautical Club to meet them. Well, nobody was more surprised than me when he offered me the job of branch manager of his estate agency business in Punta Prima, which is about 7 kilometres from the centre of Torrevieja. I was quite taken aback and asked him why me, to which he replied that he did not know anyone else in Spain that had as much managerial experience as me. I am not sure if he meant it or was simply flattering me.

I was not overly keen on the position, as it meant working a lot more hours and Saturday mornings; but when the accountant explained the package to me, I found I was unable to refuse. After a lengthy discussion, I agreed to take the job on the basis that if it did not work out then I could return to the job I had then, or retire again.

The first year it went extremely well and we were selling around 20 properties each month. As branch manager, I was paid a basic salary plus a percentage from each property sold by every member of staff. As a result, I was earning a very healthy salary and certainly a lot more than I had expected.

Payments were always cash in hand, so one had to be very careful where to keep the money – it would be unwise to put it in the bank. Banks in Spain work in a similar way to those in the UK and any regular amounts of money being deposited into an account would raise suspicion. Banks in Spain, however, generally seem more switched on to money laundering, so you'd have to be very careful not to raise suspicion. I found it was just as easy to keep the funds in the safe at home as it always appeared to be spent fast enough.

My wife and I were very lucky at the time, as we had just sold the first villa we owned in Spain and bought a 3-bedroomed villa on a 600 sq. m plot in Benijófar, just outside Quesada. We had plans to extend the villa, as there was plenty of room at the rear of the property. I wanted to put a fourth bedroom on the back of the villa and install an 8x4 swimming pool.

This is where my earnings came in very useful, paying for all the extras we wanted for the new home, such as the pool, security grills, alarm systems, air conditioning, central heating, vanity units, all the white goods, bathroom fittings and light fittings, together with a figure of around €3,000 for landscaping the garden.

We invited three builders to come and quote for the work that we desired for the new villa, including raising the boundary walls to 2.1 m with wall lights fitted every 3 m, an 8x4 m swimming pool, a fourth bedroom with an underbuild, and tiling on the patios and terraces around the house. We also decided to have lights in the pool and uplighters in some of the flower borders for the effect, together with an irrigation system. We knew we were going over the top in certain areas, but it made sense to have all the work done at once so that we could hide all the pipes and cables under the tiles.

The builders that we chose were recommended to us by a friend, who was also in the real-estate business; and whilst they were all Bulgarians, they proved to be extremely good workers and frequently woke us at 7 a.m., working through until about 8 p.m., stopping for half an hour for breakfast at 10 a.m. and an hour for lunch at 2 p.m. They only spoke Bulgarian or Russian, but Pablo (the boss) spoke eight different languages, so there was never a problem. When he initially told us he could start in a month, we asked him if he would have all the required licenses by then and he assured us that there would be no problem. He then explained that there would be a huge amount of soil to be removed from the pool area, so he would begin there, using what soil he could in levelling the garden – the rest he would dispose of elsewhere.

On the Saturday, 14 December – the day before we were due to fly back to the UK for Christmas – they arrived bright and early along with a JCB and a very large tipper truck and started to dig out the swimming pool. As Pablo had already marked out where the pool was going to go, they started digging straightaway. We flew back to the UK on Sunday, 15 December, wondering what on earth we would come back to.

We were in the UK for three weeks, a trip we managed to do two or three times a year, and when we returned we had so much luggage that Sue's sister, Terry, came back with us to ease the excess baggage charges. Apart from wanting to see the new villa, I really think that it was just an excuse for a week's break from her normal routine.

On our return, the builders had made very good progress and had finished digging out the pool, which looked enormous, and they had started to lay its foundations. They had already started to raise the height of the perimeter walls to the maximum allowed, which was 2.1 m under the local by-laws, and Pablo continued to assure us that he had the licenses, and so we let him get on with it.

We had already decided that a good enhancement to the garden would be to install lighting on the perimeter walls along with a few uplighters amongst the plants. So Pablo took us to a local electrical wholesaler where we purchased all the lighting we required at cost price.

The size of the plot on the original plans was 466 sq. m, but when Pablo's architect measured the plot he announced that we actually had 610 sq. m, so the raising of the perimeter walls was quite a job in itself. But his gang did not hang about and were almost finished when we had a visit from the *policía local* asking to see the licenses, which they knew did not exist. Once we had established with Pablo that the licenses had not yet come through, the *policía* informed us that no more work could be carried out until we had the required licences in place, making my wife sign to that effect as I was at work at the time.

I think it is worth pointing out that the *policía local* station is based at the town hall and they work very closely with the local authority. I suspect that the *policía local* had seen the work going on as they patrolled the area – which they did so very frequently – and checked with the town hall to establish whether we had the licenses to carry out the work in question. The cost of the licences (if I remember correctly) was based on a percentage of the estimated value of the construction. This was, of course, a very important source of revenue for the local authority.

Pablo came round that evening to see us and we sat on the terrace and had a bottle of wine or two while he explained the situation to us and how he proposed to resolve it. By the time Pablo and I had finished the second bottle of wine, we were both very merry, which did concern me as Pablo was driving, but the Spanish did not seem overly bothered about that sort of thing at the time. Now, however, Spain promotes a zero-tolerance policy on drink-driving. Mind you, I remember getting a right rollicking that evening because a certain person thought that it was my fault that Pablo had drank so much.

The following morning, Pablo's men arrived as normal at 7 a.m. and had parked their vehicle around the corner, out of site from the villa. They climbed down into the pool, and began tiling the interior accordingly, in the hope that the police would not be able to see them from the road. This they did for about three days, making my wife extremely nervous; she'd been having kittens every day, particularly as it was her signature on the official papers. Eventually, the licenses came though and Pablo proceeded, legally, with the extension and terracing.

Then one morning, Pablo came to us bright and early and said that he thought that we were doing it all wrong. He suggested that if we paid him another €1,500, he would dig out the area under the extension, construct a *sótano* (underbuild) and put the utility and storage area underneath the fourth bedroom. Well, as you can imagine, it did not take much consideration as it meant that we were getting an extra room effectively for €1,500. We gave the go-ahead and two of his guys dug the underbuild out by hand and built the *sótano*, which proved to be a superb enhancement to the villa.

When the pool was completed, I questioned Pablo on the cost of filling it with water; he replied that I was not to worry about it, he would take care of the matter. When he eventually filled it, I looked to see how, and to my amazement he had disconnected our water meter and connected the hosepipe directly into the main, consequently filling the pool without the water being monitored. Five years later when I did refill the pool after maintenance, the cost of refilling was €480 and I wondered if the water authority would query it, but I never heard anything from them.

Both the garden and the terraces were now completed and we had been to a large, local Spanish garden centre and purchased several trees, shrubs and various plants. When the garden was completed, we notified the garden centre and they delivered and planted what we'd chosen, as this was all included in the purchase price. All we had to do was to lay them out where we wanted them and they did the rest.

We did go slightly over budget – but nothing too serious – and, once it was all complete, it looked the business. The whole episode took a total of eight months, so we got to know all the builders quite well and were able to converse with them. If we see them out and about today, they always come over and shake our hands and ask how we are and how the garden is coming on.

Pablo and his wife, Toni, became very good friends of ours, and we often visited his wife's restaurant (known as Tyler's Bar) which was in the centre of Rojales. They were, in fact, in partnership with another English couple, and so the restaurant was known locally for its English and Bulgarian food.

However, after about two years, the partnership broke up and the bar was sold, due to the fact that the partner was not too keen on working, and so, as a result, expected Toni to work 14 hours a day. I am pleased to say that Pablo and Toni remain very close friends of mine to this day.

Around 18 months after joining the estate agency, we had a visit from the Spanish social security services, who were doing an inspection on all the businesses in the area, checking to ensure that all the employees had contracts and were registered with the social services. Well, we were caught with our trousers down good and proper, as the saying goes, as only two of the employees were legal, and six employees – including myself – were not registered on the Spanish system at all.

If you register an employee with the Spanish social security you have to provide them with a contract of employment, which meant that you had to pay social security totalling €250 for each employee per month. The individual was, however, responsible for declaring and paying his own income tax as a self-employed citizen.

We were very fortunate as the boss was a solicitor with a practice in Torrevieja. When I reported the issue to him he was not at all happy and immediately came to the office. After he had spoken to all the employees that the inspector had interviewed, he set to and bailed us all out, then registered us all the following day. Thankfully, we neither saw nor heard any more from the inspectors. Had we been summonsed, we could have been liable for a fine of €6,000 each, along with the company being fined €60,000.

To this day, I believe that an ex-employee who had been

asked to leave the company under a cloud had reported us to the social services for her revenge; but we shall never know the truth.

A few weeks later, the sales director called a meeting involving all staff. He really laid down the law on how we should be doing things, what we should be doing, and what we were to wear in the office. I did not like his attitude – the way he relayed his message in such a dictatorial manner was certainly not to my liking.

After two years with the estate agency, the business had dropped out of the housing market in Spain and another friend of mine asked me to go and work for him. This opportunity came at a good time; it would relieve me from the hassle of running the office, which was becoming very pressurised as a result of the business dropping off, and the attitude of the sales director only eoncouraged me to take another opportunity elsewhere.

So I decided to leave La Perla Estate Agency and moved to Homes España as a *vendedor* (salesman). This lasted three months, as it suddenly struck me that I was working 12 hours a day and sometimes more – if the client purchased then I would take them to dinner, not getting home until midnight. I sat down and had a lenghtly discussion with the boss and we decided that we would call it a day and that I would only work on a freelance basis.

It was around two months later that I had a call from La Perla Estates informing me that an official letter had arrived in the office from the Orihuela Court, summoning me to appear before the court on 15 December 2005. We had already booked our flights back to the UK leaving on 6 December, so I had to present myself to the clerk of the court with an interpreter explaining why we would not be able to attend, providing full documentation of proof that I was not going to be in the country. Fortunately, this was not a problem to the court, which rescheduled the case for 25 April 2006.

The case was in regards to a client whose house was on our books but had actually been sold via another agent, and I was to attend the case in court as she had cited me as a witness for her. Now the system was that the commission in cases like this would be split 50/50 with the agents involved. However, in this case, when the money was passed to the vendor by the solicitor, they gave her all the commission, leaving the two agents with nothing. The vendor was, of course, delighted and refused to return the commission to the agents. So, my now ex-boss decided to sue the vendor to recover the commission. Having been the office manager for La Perla at the time as well as being cited as a witness, this all became very complex and difficult for me.

However, the case was eventually heard about nine months later and approximately one week before the hearing, I was asked to attend a meeting with the owner of La Perla together with his lawyer to discuss the case. I wonder what the lawyer of the vendor, or even the judge, would have had to say about that, considering I was a witness for the vendor. The lawyer went through all the questions that he was going to ask me along with the answers that he wanted me to give. The lawyer instructed that I was not to hesitate with my answer and I was to say 'yes' to each question that he'd ask me. One has to bear in mind that by this time I had not been employed by La Perla for some nine months, so I felt that the scenario was not quite as bad as I'd first imagined, although I did not know where I stood legally in regards to talking to the opposition, so to speak.

The day of the hearing arrived. I drove to Orihuela Crown Court and duly waited outside the courtroom for the vendor and their lawyer to arrive, thinking he'd want to give a brief induction on the procedures of the court. Instead, however, it was quite the contrary and nobody spoke to me at all. I saw two young ladies walk into the court in jeans and T-shirts, each with a cloak over their arms. I thought no more of it until the clerk of the court called us in and, lo and behold, there were the two young ladies sitting at the bench in their robes over the top of their casual clothes. They realized I was a witness, and I was ushered out of the courtroom and informed that I would be called upon when required. At this stage I was, as you can imagine, nervous as hell. I'd never been in court before (save for my divorce) and now I was in a court of a foreign country, unable to speak the native language and wondering what the format was going to be.

Eventually, I was called into the courtroom and through an interpreter the judge warned me that I was under oath and that the penalties were severe if I told porky pies.

The first question she asked was whether I worked for La Perla Estates; I obviously had to say no, as I had left some nine months previously. She then asked me if I had previously worked for La Perla and if so, to confirm the dates of my employment. I replied that yes, I had been employed by La Perla and stated the dates, to which the whole court looked at one another – the dates I had given did not compare with the paperwork that had been submitted to the court. After the judge had consulted with the clerk of the court, she beckoned me to the bench for further clarification on the matter.

The judge then quietly spoke to me in very good English and asked me to identify several papers along with the signatures on each page and asked me if I believed them to be authentic. I confirmed that the signatures were valid and the judge asked me to name the members of staff that the signatures belonged to, which I did.

It then dawned on me that the questions the lawyer of La Perla Estates was proposing to ask me required a 'yes' answer, yet here I was replying 'no' to all the questions so far, which really put the cat amongst the pigeons with my ex-employer.

However, through an interpreter, both lawyers asked me a few questions that I duly replied to truthfully. Finally, the judge decided she had heard enough for the time being and announced that she would not give a ruling until she had heard from the purchaser, who was not in court, to establish and confirm that the figures involved were in fact correct. Some 18 months later, I learned that the vendor won the case, leaving my ex-employer losing out to the tune of €12,000 plus costs.

On 16 August 2005 I received a phone call from my brother telling me that Mother had suffered another fall and was in the John Radcliffe Hospital, Oxford with a suspected broken thigh. The JR had difficulties concluding what had been broken, and put Mother on a standby list, which meant that emergencies came first. Eight days later, Mother still hadn't even been given a diagnosis, so my sister-in-law complained and reminded them of their duty of care. They finally managed to x-ray the leg, which confirmed that it was broken, and the following day Mother underwent corrective surgery.

Bearing in mind that Mother was 94, she had suffered so much pain over the last couple of weeks that unfortunately she did not recover from the operation and passed away in the early hours of the morning.

I booked a flight home on the Wednesday and the funeral was held on the Thursday at the Methodist Church in Abingdon and the cemetery in Spring Road, Abingdon, where she was buried alongside Dad. Mother had purchased a double grave when my father died so that they could one day be buried together. After saying a final farewell, we all went to the Four Pillars Hotel, also in Abingdon, for a buffet with friends and relatives.

Today, I am once again retired and trying to keep myself busy around the house and garden. I also visit a local dog sanctuary for homeless and abandoned dogs and take five or six of them for a walk two or three times every week. It is extremely good exercise for this temple of mine, which I try to look after as best as I can (taking into account the abuse it gets from the red wine and the Spanish brandy).

The sanctuary houses around 90 dogs. Some have actually been very well looked after throughout their lives, but left homeless when their owners returned to their native land. Some have been abandoned by their owners and left in a very poor condition; a few of them so bad their ribs poke through their skin. We have a number of dogs that are suffering from Leishmaniasis, which is a form of HIV in canines and is transmitted via mosquitoes. There are some very sad cases there, though I get a certain amount of pleasure gained from helping both the sanctuary and the dogs.

Now that I have retired, I do play a lot more golf with several friends, and I have also joined a couple of golf societies, with whom I play twice a month on 12 different courses during the course of the year, the farthest being about one hour's drive. I did get my handicap down to 19, but it has gone back up to 22 again since I have not been playing quite so much these days.

I decided not to join a golf club as I already have the luxury of around 40 courses in the area where I live, all within one hour's drive. Usually a group of us will play one or two different courses each week. Golf in Spain is very different from the UK, with the courses in the main championships and very picturesque; more often than not the courses are lined with palm, olive or almond trees, with lots more bunkers, lakes or water hazards on the fairways. They are probably 1,000 m longer than you'd fine in the UK and the ground is much harder, so you do not take many divots, and, in fairness, the ball probably runs a lot further.

On 6 May 2007, my wife started a new job in the UK caring for the elderly in their own homes. The assignment was for three weeks, but she decided to spend a few days with her sister before the assignment started, as well as a few days afterwards.

She was away for a total of five weeks, returning on 3 June. On her return to Spain, I noted all was not well by the coldness of her reception. The following day, I suggested that it would be nice to have some friends over who had been kind to me in her absence, to which she suddenly said that she did not want to be in Spain at all.

I admitted that I had guessed something was wrong and that I felt that there was more to come. With that, she turned to me and said that being away for five weeks had made her realize that she did not love me anymore and that I would not feature in her future life. As you can imagine, I was dumbfounded and quite lost for words.

The next day I played golf and I thought about what she had said. I decided that I had to put up a fight – I could not let my third marriage slip away just like that, after 25 years of being together. So, on my return home, I put forward several suggestions to her, whereby I compromised in a lot of areas so that we could at least stay together. We had reached a stage in our lives where we had invested well; Sue was drawing on a couple of private pensions and I was drawing my Citroën pension. We also had other pensions, which together were very good. I was about to draw my state pension. All in all, we would be very comfortable in our twilight years, so it made a lot of sense to stay together.

24 Heures du Mans 2007

In April of this year, I had been in communication with Dave Cato, who organized a trip to Le Mans each year for a group of Citroën employees and the dealer network. He had invited me several times to join them, as he knew I was a fan of Le Mans and had, of course, attended on a couple of the previously described occasions. I was anxious to do the Le Mans thing one more time, so, in response to the invitation, I discussed the trip with a great friend of mine, Maurice, and we both agreed to drive from Spain to the event. We also arranged to meet another friend there with whom I had attended the event several times before.

On 14 June, Maurice and I set off for the 24 Heures du Mans, held just southwest of Paris. In an attempt to shave some time off the journey, we took with us a couple of cool boxes filled with food and drink, and planned to drive for around 14 hours each day, with one stop overnight in a hotel on route.

We did not want to leave the ladies at home without transport, so we decided to take my SEAT León and arranged for my wife to borrow Maurice's car, while Maurice's wife borrowed a friend's until we returned.

Our route took us up to Valencia, then on to Barcelona. From there, we made our way north towards the French border and Perpignan, then on towards Toulouse, where we stayed the night in a nice, clean, cheap hotel, had a few brandies in the evening and then went to bed where we slept like two babies.

The following day, we left the hotel at about 8.30 a.m. feeling refreshed and raring to go. We continued on the autoroute and headed for Bordeaux, Poitiers and then Tours. Once we reached Tours, we headed for a small town called Sées just north of Le Mans, where we met up with a couple of pals from the UK, Ron and Alan, at Hotel La Daphne. Ron and I had frequented this hotel on several occasions when visiting Le Mans, so it was very familiar to us. That evening we had a great meal accompanied by a nice bottle of red wine and a glass of quality Cognac before going to bed.

At breakfast, we were presented with the bill and were shocked, to say the least, to find that the Cognac was €25 a glass. We were extremely relieved that we had only had one each.

We eventually left the hotel around 8.45 a.m. to drive south to Le Mans, which we knew would take just over an hour depending on the traffic. The road structure had changed dramatically (for the better, I might add) in the two years since I was last there, so it was a question of getting to know the place once again.

We eventually picked up the route that led us to a very congested car park and found our allocated space. We then made our way down to the main entrance of the circuit and on to the grandstand that we had reserved and where we had planned on meeting the party from Citroën.

It was around 11 a.m. when we arrived and the grandstand was virtually empty, so we used this to our advantage and as we had heard that there had been a lot of modernization made to the 'village' as it was known, we wandered about to see what changes had been made. To our amazement, the village had been completely demolished and rebuilt again. Everything had changed – it was now very modern but lacked the atmosphere and character we once enjoyed

We returned to the grandstand and were promptly greeted by Dave Cato, who had very kindly organized the trip for the UK contingent as well as the tickets for Maurice and me. Dave, I might add, was one of the people who had convinced me to write this autobiography.

The rest of the party from Citroën had also arrived, and it was nice to see some old faces and catch up with all that was new in their lives. I had, of course, seen one or two of them recently, but I had always enjoyed catching up with all the gossip from the lads and meeting new faces.

The race this year was an interesting one, with the Audi Peugeot diesels dominating the race entirely. The Audis took the lead from the first lap in 1st and 2nd position, with Peugeot 3rd and 4th and that is how it remained for most of the race. However, during the night, one of the Audis crashed and, a little while later, one of the Peugeots retired.

On Saturday evening, Maurice and I decided to sleep in the

car and were both amazed at how well we slept, only being woken by my bladder telling me it was time to get up at 6.30 a.m.

We both rose at the same time and breakfast was served from our trusty cool box, before wandering down to the circuit with Ron and Alan to look for somewhere to get some coffee. We found a bar which suited our needs perfectly, then headed back to the grandstand to meet up with the other guys and to get an update on what we had missed during the night.

We sauntered through the different areas of the circuit in an attempt to view the race from various angles, and then at around 1 p.m. we noticed heavy black clouds coming our way. We had already noted the weather forecast over the closed-circuit television, which predicted heavy rain later in the day. So Maurice and I decided that we should return to the car and commence our journey home. We said all our goodbyes to Dave and the boys and made our way back to the car park, leaving the circuit at around 1.30 p.m. for the journey back to Spain.

About 15 minutes into our drive, the heavens opened and we crawled along the autoroute at about 40km an hour. The rain had also necessitated bringing the pace car out for the remainder of the race, so by leaving early we missed absolutely nothing.

We made very good time despite the weather, and stopped at one of the larger service stations located along the autoroute where we had a shower and a bite to eat before continuing our journey, discussing where we should take our overnight stop.

Finally, we agreed that as we had slept so well the night before in the car, we would carry on motoring and get as far as we could, then stop in a safe place and sleep in the car again. After crossing the border into Spain, we motored for another hour and when we were approximately 120km from Barcelona we pulled into a huge lay-by, where there were several other stationary vehicles, and had something to eat before settling down for the night.

The following day we woke at around 6 a.m. and drove 15 minutes to the next service station, where we replenished ourselves with breakfast, had a quick wash and brushed our teeth. Again we motored on, taking one more comfort break, and after a very good run we arrived back in Benijofar at about 4.30 p.m. Maurice dropped me off at my villa and drove back to his in Campoverde, where Sue would be waiting to switch vehicles before returning home.

It was clear that not all was well within our relationship, and a week later Sue returned to the UK while I stayed in Spain. I had already accepted a rental on the villa for the duration of the last week of June with our rental agency, Overseas Property Investments, so it was necessary to find somewhere alternative to stay. I telephoned my pal, Phil, and arranged to rent his apartment opposite the Naufragos beach in Torrevieja for one week.

While I was there, I made full use of the time to do some research on writing this autobiography filling in some of the details that I had struggled to remember. In the evenings, I would have dinner at around 7 p.m. before walking down to the local bar for a drink and watching the football on the TV with the Spanish locals. At the time I did not speak Spanish very well, however, they seemed to welcome me with open arms and understood me more than I understood them.

I had been renting Phil's apartment for four days when I got a call from my Aunt Vera in Scotland, saying that she had been diagnosed with pancreatic cancer and did not have much time to live. My aunt had always been very good at exaggerating, so I contacted the doctor in charge of the ward and explained that I was her next of kin and that I lived in Spain, and needed to know how much time I had to return. He advised me that, as her next of kin, I should get back to the UK as soon as possible. Without hesitation, I got myself organized and drove to Alicante airport the next day to book a flight to Scotland so that I could be there for her. I also phoned one of her friends in Tranent, which was roughly 12 miles from the centre of Edinburgh where my aunt lived and arranged for one of the family to collect me from Edinburgh airport.

My aunt had also phoned Sue with the news, completely oblivious of our marriage difficulties, and that was how it remained – I felt that there was no need to tell her at this point in her life.

I flew into Edinburgh on 1 July, the day after the car bomb had gone off at Glasgow Airport. So, as you can imagine, the security at the airport was on red alert, which meant that no vehicles could get within three miles of the airport.

George Thompson, who was a very close friend of Vera's, was due to pick me up, but, he was, of course, stuck in the traffic surrounding the airport. After consulting with the family, it was decided that I should take the shuttle bus to the park-and-ride and sort it out from there. We finally arranged to meet at the Hilton Hotel on the Corstorphine Road, which was on the outskirts of Edinburgh.

George took me back to Vera's house, for which, fortunately, I had a set of keys and would be staying for the duration. I unpacked and pottered around until George arrived at 6 p.m. to drive us both to the hospital in Edinburgh. I had been in contact with Sue and I had told her which bus to catch and where to get off, and explained to her that George and I would meet her and take us straight to the hospital to see Vera.

Vera was absolutely over the moon to see us; she had not known when we would arrive, due to the difficulty in getting through to her on the oncology ward. Sue and I stuck to the plan of not telling Vera about our separation, as she thought we had the perfect marriage and the idea of us separating would have upset her. To this day I regret that I deceived my aunt and all her friends throughout the time she had remaining. I actually felt very guilty about it afterwards and made my apologies to some of her friends.

Sue and I stayed in Vera's house in Tranent for three months. We had separate rooms and were almost living separate lives; but during this time we visited Vera every day, and on numerous occasions twice a day. During our stay, we had the use of her car. I was already a_named driver on the policy and this made it easier for us to visit Vera without difficulty.

I knew that Vera had left the property to me and that it required some tender loving care. It had not been decorated for 15 years, many of which were also spent accommodating at least four canine companions. I knew that it would take me some time to renovate inside and out, including the garden; so I took the opportunity to start decorating straightaway, helping me swerve the difficulties of being in the same house with Sue and keeping my mind diverted from thinking about our marital situation. I also cleared and cleaned the garage, which was in an awful state and took many trips to the local dump to clear it.

On 3 August, Vera told the hospital she wanted to go home and said she had us to look after her. So without consulting us, they decided to discharge Vera with a package of home help. It quickly became very clear to us that the main responsibility was on the shoulders of Sue and me to look after her. No matter what we said to try to increase the home help, it did not seem to make any difference. Our pleas falling on deaf ears, the authorities would not increase the package, and it became very clear to me that their priority was to get her out of the hospital, freeing up a hospital bed.

Vera had a nurse that came in twice a day to look after her personal needs, however, it became clear after three or four days that the nurse was having great difficulty in coping with her. Vera was a big lady, twice the size of her nurse, who was unable to lift her on her own, and so she asked her boss for assistance.

The following morning, the nurse was unable to help her off the toilet on her own, so Sue had to assist her. As a result, we arranged a meeting with social services who came to the house to assess her situation and discuss her case. It was decided that the time had come to move her bed into the lounge in a position where two nurses could access either side of the bed, enabling them to do whatever they needed to. We moved her bed into the lounge, rearranged the furniture, and moved the television into a better position so that she had something to watch all day. The bed also had to be in the correct position so that she could watch the birds in the garden in the feeding boxes that I filled every morning with birdseed.

As time went by, we realized that eventually we would not be able to cope, because she was trying to get out of bed and her legs were unable to carry her weight. Sue and I decided that it was necessary for one of us to sleep downstairs to ensure Vera did not attempt to get out of bed. We planned a four-hour rota system where we would sleep in her reclining chair, listening for any movement from Vera. Two days later, we called the doctor in – it was impossible for the nurses and ourselves to cope any longer in that environment and we told him that we could not manage anymore, that we were totally out of our depth, and that he must do something to help Vera. He promptly got on the phone and found her a bed in the Marie Curie Hospice in Edinburgh. An ambulance was at the house within half an hour to take her there, where she was finally made comfortable in the hospice within the hour.

She did not like the hospice, but accepted that she needed care and that she did not have long to live. Two days after she had arrived at the hospice, and completely out of the blue, she asked me if I knew what to do when she was gone, to which I reassured her that I did. She told me that I should go and make a start on planning, as she did not want us to see her suffering in her last few days.

Though we visited on several occasions, she was often asleep or under medication and completely unaware that we were there. On a particular visit one Friday morning, the sister called us into her office and told us that Vera had endured a very restless night and they thought that the end was very close now. They even offered us beds for the night so that we were on site should something happen. We told the sister that it was Vera's wish for us not to see her suffer and declined the bed. Later that evening we got a call from the hospice informing us that Vera was not going to last the night and if we wanted to change our minds about the bed then the hospice would arrange it.

Unfortunately, later that evening, at 11.30 p.m. to be precise, and four days after Vera arrived at the hospice on 17 August, I got the call to say that she had passed away in her sleep. As next of kin, I was asked to go into the hospice the following morning to sign some papers and collect her belongings.

There was, however, a very strange happening on the night Vera passed away. Shortly after I had the call from the hospice, Vera's friend from Miami called me, as she did most nights for an update on Vera. Vera had exported three cocker spaniels to this lady a couple of years previous, and they had always stayed in touch. The friend mentioned that her dogs had gone crazy at around 11.15 p.m. and would not stop barking, so much so that she even called the police thinking there may be an intruder on her land – but the police could find no one. I informed her that Vera had passed away around this time, and we both wondered if the dogs had sensed the passing of Vera.

Another of my duties as next of kin and the executor was to organize both the funeral and the wake. Vera had given me certain instructions as to what she wanted and who I was to invite before she left us.

The funeral took place eight days later at the Edinburgh Crematorium on the east side of town, and apart from two of my cousins, Stuart and Jennifer, no other family member was present to support Sue and I at the funeral, which I have to admit greatly disappointed me.

We had arranged the wake in the function room of a local pub in Tranent, where we had taken Vera for a meal on numerous occasions. George and Sue Thompson were close friends of Vera's, and George's daughter, Samantha, worked at the pub at weekends. She was an enormous help to me with the organization of the wake, making sure that everything was how I wanted, even down to arranging some Isle of Jura malt whisky on the day as I felt that I would surely need it.

I had already spoken with the solicitor to get things moving with putting the house on the market, but apparently we had to wait until the Scottish court gave us the authority to sell the property. This was something that was organized during probate and whilst there was a will, it still goes through probate in Scotland.

This was achieved by the end of December, allowing Murdo Tait (Vera's solicitor) and an estate agent to begin marketing the property. By now, the house was decorated throughout with new carpets in every room including the hall, stairs, and landing, and during the course of our final week there we removed the rest of the furniture. I found Murdo to be a smashing fellow and we got on extremely well; we continued to communicate via email once I had left Scotland.

Most of the furniture and the items that we did not want were donated to the PDSA charity organization, as Vera had worked with them in the past and supported them as much as she could, and this was one of her instructions given to me. The PDSA charity organization had a couple of shops in Edinburgh and Vera had worked in the Musselberry store, which was only about ten minutes from her home in the car.

At the end of September, Sue and I took a domestic flight to Gatwick and stayed for one week with Sue's sister in Farnborough before flying back to Spain. Sue had decided that she would return with me to collect her belongings. Once we arrived in Spain, Sue started packing most of the clothes that she wanted to take back with her to England for the oncoming English winter.

I was quite emotional at this stage, so I decided that I had to take a positive attitude to all this or else I would become a nervous wreck within a week. One of my friends had told me that once I had got rid of all the emotions, something good would come of it.

It was a difficult for time for me and on top of it all I found I was becoming a slave to the property and enquired about a cleaner. However, it was a big villa and all the cleaners wanted too much money to clean it, so I decided that it was down to me to keep it clean.

After a couple of months, I looked around and joined a couple of diners clubs for single people. These clubs met once a week, usually on a Friday. We frequented a different restaurant every week, where we would have a good chinwag over dinner and a dance afterwards. It gave me the opportunity to get to know a few people and date any of the ladies that were present if they took my fancy. Usually, it was not until I took a lady out alone that I'd get to really know her, and sometimes it would become apparent that she was not what I was looking for. The first time I attended as a club member, I took a shine to one particular lady; but unfortunately she was already spoken for, so I decided to bide my time in other ways.

The following April, it was my 65th birthday and I decided to organize a dinner party at a restaurant nearby. I had two restaurants in mind, so I talked to both to see which one could offer me the best package. One was in Guardamar, which was about 12 kilometres from the villa; and the other was in Almoradi, about the same distance from home. I decided to settle for the one in Guardamar as it was a larger venue and, I thought, more professional. The manager was prepared to arrange for me a three-course meal with a choice of five dishes, with a glass of champagne on arrival and a glass to accompany each course. I was happy with the cost I was paying for the meal, while the guests would pay for their own drinks.

A few days before my birthday, my eldest son phoned me and told me that they would be arriving in Spain a couple of days before my party, which was fabulous news as I would otherwise not have had any family there at all.

I had invited about 20 people in all, so this pushed the number up to 24. The restaurant had arranged the table in a U shape, enabling me to socialize with everyone from my seat. My two grandchildren chose to sit next to a Russian lady, who was the girlfriend of a friend of mine, and she entertained them all night drawing and colouring for them; they loved it. It was a superb night and all my guests enjoyed it and I certainly did too.

As the months went by, I had joined a couple of dating sites but I seemed to be getting nowhere The main one being Club Amistad, a Chilean dating site that had a variety of ladies situated all over the world, most of them from South America. I had not been very lucky with English ladies in the past, so I decided to try ladies of different nationalities. There were two that I was smitten with: a Russian lady and a Brazilian lady.

The Russian lady lived locally and we dated several times

and enjoyed each other's company, but the chemistry was missing. It was a shame, as she was a lovely lady, around 38 with blonde hair, blue eyes, a full figure and a super personality and sense of humour. She also had two teenage daughters who were both at a local school, but, unfortunately, there did not seem to be any chemistry between us either.

The Brazilian lady was different to other ladies I'd dated in the past, and I did not believe that I stood a chance. However, I decided to persevere and see where it would take me, as I was in no rush to be attached again. Now, she had black hair and dark eyes, again, a very full figure, more mature at the age of around 54 and she had two sons and a daughter, the youngest being 21 years old.

After several months of chatting each night on the Internet, it appeared that we were getting on quite well. So it was a matter of taking it a stage further and we decided to arrange a meeting to see if we were compatible and if we wanted to continue with the relationship. At the time she lived in Denmark, which was not that far away. So we decided to share the cost of her flight to Spain for a long weekend.

It was late in November 2008 when she flew to Alicante. I picked her up from the airport and the next four days were spent getting to know each other and see what we had in common, and if there was any chemistry between us. Well, as it appeared, the chemistry was overflowing on both sides and we were both very keen to carry on with the relationship.

Maybe this is a good place to stop. As I hope you will see, my 65 years have been adventurous. I've certainly had my trials and tribulations, but I've also had the privilege of meeting many wonderful people, particularly throughout my career, which brought me many fond memories. This book ends leaving blank pages ready to be filled — maybe the next ten years will be as exciting as the first 65.

The End. For Now.

Made in the USA
Charleston, SC
09 June 2016